STARTING WI

Continuum's *Starting with ...* series offers clear, concise and accessible introductions to the key thinkers in philosophy. The books explore and illuminate the roots of each philosopher's work and ideas, leading readers to a thorough understanding of the key influences and philosophical foundations from which his or her thought developed. Ideal for first-year students starting out in philosophy, the series will serve as the ideal companion to study of this fascinating subject.

Available now:

Starting with Berkeley, Nick Jones

Starting with Derrida, Sean Gaston

Starting with Descartes, C.G. Prado

Starting with Hegel, Craig B. Matarrese

Starting with Heidegger, Tom Greaves

Starting with Hobbes, George MacDonald Ross

Starting with Leibniz, Roger Woolhouse

Starting with Mill, John R. Fitzpatrick

Starting with Nietzsche, Ullrich Haase

Starting with Rousseau, James Delaney

Starting with Sartre, Gail Linsenbard

Forthcoming:

Starting with Hume, Charlotte R. Brown and
    William Edward Morris

Starting with Kant, Andrew Ward

Starting with Kierkegaard, Patrick Sheil

Starting with Merleau-Ponty, Katherine Morris

Starting with Wittgenstein, Chon Tejedor

STARTING WITH LOCKE

GREG FORSTER

continuum

Continuum International Publishing Group
The Tower Building   80 Maiden Lane
11 York Road   Suite 704
London SE1 7NX   New York, NY 10038

www.continuumbooks.com

British Library Cataloguing-in-Publication Data
A catalogue record for this book is available from the British Library.

ISBN: HB: 978–1–8470–6582–7
PB: 978–1–8470–6583–4

Library of Congress Cataloging-in-Publication Data
Forster, Greg, 1973–
Starting with Locke / Greg Forster.
p. cm.
ISBN 978–1–84706–582–7 – ISBN 978–1–84706–583–4
1. Locke, John, 1632–1704. I. Title.

B1296.F67 2010
192–dc22

2010018300

Typeset by RefineCatch Limited, Bungay, Suffolk
Printed and bound in India by Replika Press Pvt Ltd

John Locke is the most influential philosopher of modern times.
– Hans Aarsleff, "Locke's Influence"
(in *The Cambridge Companion to Locke*)

CONTENTS

CONTENTS

ACKNOWLEDGMENTS

This book is dedicated to the generation of scholars who have transformed our understanding of Locke in the past half-century by restoring our knowledge of how he was shaped by, and shaped, the titanic struggles of his times. For nearly two centuries, Locke had been reduced to a dry peddler of airy abstractions. It has been a long, slow process restoring an appreciation of what was really at stake for Locke and why he was once thought so important. But the effort has been rewarded; the real, historical Locke seems now to be established, at least among those paying attention to Locke studies, beyond much dispute. The larger intellectual world may not yet have met this real Locke, a problem with which I hope I may offer some help; but the task of digging up and reconstructing the real Locke was much harder than the present task of putting him on display. I'm grateful to acknowledge how deeply I've benefited from the path-breaking work of my predecessors.

I wish to express my additional gratitude to the teachers who guided me as I undertook my first studies of Locke in graduate school – Steven Smith, Norma Thompson, and Nicholas Wolterstorff chief among them; to the peers who have worked with me since then, especially Glenn Moots and Kim Ian Parker; to those who have shared knowledge and encouragement, especially Paul Sigmund and John Marshall; to my employers and colleagues at the Kern Family Foundation; to my infinitely supportive wife Beth and my daughter Anya; to all my friends and family; and above all to God.

A Word about the Text

Locke's original text is often difficult for twenty-first-century readers unaccustomed to reading seventeenth-century English. I have therefore followed the usual practice of modernizing the text in matters such as spelling, capitalization, and italicization. For increased clarity, I have also modernized its punctuation.

List of Abbreviations

References to Locke's four most important works are noted in parentheses with a capital letter followed by section and page references, as specified below. Note that section references vary in some editions of Locke's works.

Essay Concerning Human Understanding
The letter E followed by book, chapter, and paragraph numbers, followed after a comma by the page number in the Oxford edition (ed. Peter Nidditch, New York: Oxford University Press, 1979).

For example, (E IV.10.1, 619) refers to Book IV, Chapter 10, Paragraph 1 of the *Essay*, found on page 619 in the Oxford edition.

Letter Concerning Toleration
The letter L followed by the paragraph number, followed after a comma by the page number in the Prentice-Hall edition (ed. Patrick Romanell, Englewood Cliffs, NJ: Prentice-Hall, 1950).

For example, (L 37, 31) refers to Paragraph 37 of the *Letter*, found on page 31 of the Prentice-Hall edition.

Two Treatises of Government
The letter T followed by treatise and section numbers, followed after a comma by the page number in the Everyman edition (ed. Mark Goldie, London: Everyman, 1993).

For example, (T I.88, 63) refers to Section 88 of the *First Treatise*, found on page 63 of the Everyman edition.

The Reasonableness of Christianity as Delivered in the Scriptures
The letter R followed by the paragraph number, followed after a comma by the page number in the Regnery edition (ed. George Ewing, Washington, DC: Regnery, 1965).

For example, (R 242, 172–173) refers to Paragraph 242 of the *Reasonableness*, found on pp. 172–173 of the Regnery edition.

INTRODUCTION

This book is about the philosopher who, more than any other single person, made our world. In 1660, at age 27, looking back on the unspeakable horrors of the English Civil War and the tumults and convulsions that had followed it, he wrote: "I no sooner perceived myself in the world but I found myself in a storm which has lasted almost hitherto."[1] That storm – violent political chaos fueled primarily by religion – would continue raging for most of his life.

But by his death in 1704 the storm had been calmed, at least in England, largely by the influence of a political movement in which he was the guiding intellectual figure. And the new reconciliation of religion and politics that his thought had organized would spread beyond England, and would ultimately define the form of social order we call "modernity."[2]

John Locke stands at the turning point between the end of the Middle Ages and the emergence of the modern world. In many ways, he himself is the hinge on which the world turned. Scholars have spent a lot of time debating whether Locke should be understood as essentially a late medieval thinker or an early modern one.[3] The truth is, he's both. Throughout his writings you can see that his thinking was produced by the intellectual currents of the late medieval period. Yet those same writings changed those intellectual currents and helped modernity emerge.

One Locke scholar writes that when he read the second half of Book IV of Locke's *Essay Concerning Human Understanding*, "I felt myself present at the making of the modern mind."[4] But, to a large extent, it was a medieval mind that helped make modernity.

i. EVERYTHING OLD IS NEW – LOCKE'S CONTINUING RELEVANCE

Because Locke lived in that unique transition period when the world was moving from the medieval to the modern, you might think his philosophy would be less relevant to our own time. After all, many other seventeenth-century philosophers – René Descartes, Thomas Hobbes, Francis Bacon, Baruch Spinoza, Blaise Pascal, Gottfried Leibniz – were also, in their different ways, products of late medieval thought who helped to produce modernity. Yet few now turn to their works for answers to twenty-first-century questions.

However, Locke is different. It's true that all philosophers choose which questions to focus on based partly on the problems that are most urgent in their own times, and this can limit the relevance of their writings for readers in other time periods. But sometimes the urgent problems of one historical period speak directly to the urgent problems of another. The particular questions Locke chose to focus on make his philosophy not less relevant to our own situation, but more so.

All of Locke's major works aim squarely at solving one large problem – the catastrophic breakdown of social consensus about the intersection of religion, morality, and politics. In England in the second half of the seventeenth century, nearly two centuries of religious hatred and conflict had culminated in a period of frequent political and social upheavals, punctuated by intermittent bouts of extremely severe violence. Not just his political philosophy, but also his theology and even his technical philosophy (especially epistemology, the study of knowledge) were focused on finding a way to pacify these conflicts for the long term.

While the state of things at the beginning of the twenty-first century is not catastrophic, as it was in seventeenth-century England, the parallels between Locke's problems and our own should be clear. The English-speaking world is in a period of deep division over religious belief and its role in society and politics. And internationally, large-scale religious violence is one of our most urgent problems. Locke's success in helping people of mutually hostile religious beliefs build a common citizenship, and addressing the threat to the political order from violence motivated by religion, should be of great interest to us.

ii. THE TECTONIC PLATES – RELIGION, MORALITY, AND POLITICS

The catastrophe in late seventeenth-century England occurred because its political and social institutions had been designed in the context of a religiously homogeneous society. These institutions presupposed that the English nation as a whole both should and would share a common religion. Thus, when England came to be divided by persistent religious fragmentation, its political and social institutions became severely dysfunctional.

Locke believed the underlying problem was a failure of philosophy. People hadn't thought carefully enough about the relationship between three distinct but interconnected spheres: religious belief, moral order, and political authority. In some cases the problem was mere careless ignorance; in other cases, people had actually deceived themselves into believing that their own desires (whatever those happened to be) were really God's will. Either way, Locke was convinced that a clearer philosophical understanding of the real relationships between the religious, moral, and political spheres – and a firm determination to put that clearer understanding into practice even if it meant painful sacrifice – would yield a dramatic change for the better.

The spread of his ideas was a critical factor in the emergence of modernity. First England, then other western societies, and then ultimately a substantial portion of the world, reconceptualized the relationship between religion, morality, and politics along broadly Lockean lines. Wherever this change occurred, the consequences reverberated into every corner of society and in every aspect of human life.

From the earliest human civilizations up through the Middle Ages, it was almost universally agreed that a political community had to have a shared religion in order to survive. There cannot be shared life without shared rules, so a political community cannot exist without a set of moral laws to guide its common life – at the most basic level, rules forbidding things like murder and theft. And our knowledge of these moral rights and wrongs comes to us not from examination of the physical world, but from an awareness of something that is more than physical – something metaphysical. So a person's religion, or lack thereof, cannot help but have an impact on that person's morality.

The premodern belief that a community had to have a shared religion did not mean there was no tolerance at all for other religions. Sometimes communities tolerated religious minorities for various reasons – to facilitate international trade, to make it easier to expand an empire, out of genuine goodwill toward others, or just because persecution was costly and toleration was easier.

But even where there was toleration for religious minorities, the official community religion was always understood to be the proper basis of community life – from the broad outlines of social structure down to the details of political policy. This was simply assumed to be necessary, because the community needed to look *somewhere* for a moral basis to guide it. Thus, whenever a minority religion threatened the dominance of the community religion, suppressing it was understood to be the right thing to do in order to preserve the community.

During the Middle Ages there had been some tentative softening of this principle. As early as the turn of the fifth century, at a time when the relationship between church and state was a subject of intense controversy, Augustine – perhaps the most important theologian in Christian history – had written that "no one is ... to be compelled to embrace the faith against his will."[5] He conceived of politics in terms of the moral nature that God had put into all people, by which each person is "drawn by the laws of his nature, so to speak, to enter upon a fellowship with all his fellow-men and to keep the peace with them, as far as lies in him."[6] Later theologians developed the concept of "natural law" from these ideas, arguing that the fundamental basis of politics is not faith or the Bible, but the moral order of justice, which is known by all people through reason and conscience and is therefore shared among all human beings.[7]

But no prominent thinkers or political leaders followed these principles consistently to their logical conclusions. The fear of social disorder arising from religious pluralism was too great, and the desire to turn all means toward encouraging people to embrace the true faith was too zealous. So even while they contemplated a universal basis for the political order, they continued to support having criminal laws to punish religious offenses like blasphemy, heresy, and apostasy.

iii. THE EARTHQUAKE – THE REFORMATION AND THE WARS OF RELIGION

All that began to change when the Reformation divided European communities along religious lines. The premodern view that politics must rely on the community's shared religion had presupposed that the community would always have a shared religion. Before the Reformation, it had been relatively easy to believe that all Christians were following the same faith and that what was then called simply "the church" was its institutional voice. Not even the great schism between the western (Roman) and eastern (Orthodox) church hierarchies had shaken people's underlying confidence that there was, at bottom, only one church and only one Christian religion.

But after Martin Luther published his challenges to the Roman Catholic understanding of the gospel, it was no longer clear whether the community really had a shared faith – or who had rightful authority to say what that faith entailed. With astonishing speed, first Germany, then Switzerland, then Sweden, then England, and then France, Scotland and the Netherlands – the bulk of Europe – experienced massive popular Protestant movements. These movements did not always reach a majority of the population. But in every case they were large enough to eliminate the easy assumption that the political community would remain religiously unanimous.

In itself, this change was purely religious and not political. The differences between Protestant and Catholic theology did not concern political matters, and in fact a great variety of political opinions flourished on both sides of the religious divide. So it was not in itself a political issue which theology you held.

Nonetheless, because people thought politics should rely on the community's shared religion, the religious change had immediate and drastic political consequences. If church and state are interdependent, then any challenge to the church is also a challenge to the state. Saying that all heretics should be branded criminals and punished was one thing when only a tiny number of people were considered heretics; it was quite another when the whole population was divided in half and each side viewed the other as heretical.

Thus, the Reformation was followed by a two-century period characterized by political strife, disorder, assassinations, mob violence, oppressive enforcement of various orthodoxies, and periodic religious wars. Even if you were the sort of person who didn't have any interest in persecuting those on the other side of the religious divide, you had to worry that those on the other side would be persecuting *you* if they ever managed to get into a position of uncontested power. So there was a strong incentive to use every means necessary to seize the upper hand in every situation. Even when some kind of truce could be kept, Protestants and Catholics maintained at best an uneasy coexistence. And such truces were often facilitated by forcing religious dissenters to move out of their homes and resettle somewhere else, where their views were less objectionable, so that the religious homogeneity of the community could be maintained.

The tumults were especially bad in England, where the throne passed from Catholic to Protestant and back over and over again, sometimes rapidly. Whoever controlled the throne would seek to stamp out the other side, or at least oppress them severely enough to keep them marginalized. The fact that power was changing hands so frequently made the incentives for violence and exploitation all the stronger – any time you got into power you had to take maximum advantage of that situation while you still could.

Ironically, however, this same dynamic meant that the incentives to find a solution to the problem of religious violence were stronger in England than anywhere else. Even in Europe, people eventually do get tired of living in a constant state of bloodshed and fear. At some point they find themselves ready to try something else – even something radical – if it might help end the violence. And it was in England, where the violence was worst, that this readiness first reached a critical mass.

iv.   THE NEW WAY

The radical alternative was as simple as it was drastic. It was to unite the political community around a shared moral order without trying to unite it in religion. The moral rules that society needs to survive (don't kill, don't steal, keep your promises, help your neighbors) are not tied to a particular religion. Protestants and Catholics were generally agreed about such moral rules, and for that matter so were members of most other religions. If I believe in the rules of fair play because I'm Protestant and you believe in them because you're Catholic, the important thing is that we both believe in the rules of fair play, not what religion teaches us to believe in them.[8]

People realized that in fact, by far the biggest obstacle to fair play between members of different religious groups was precisely that they kept persecuting each other over religion. The old philosophy said society needed a shared religion in order to maintain its shared moral rules. But, ironically, this very quest for a shared religion had itself become the biggest threat to the shared moral rules.

As obvious as all this may seem to us now, we must remember how radical it was at the time. The idea did have roots in a thousand years' worth of development in Christian natural law theory. But it had never been taken all the way to its logical conclusion before. To most people, saying that the community could have shared moral rules without a shared religion was a little like saying you could drive around in a carriage without any horses to draw it. Everyone thinks it's impossible – until someone invents the automobile.

Another reason this radical idea hadn't been tried before was fear of what might happen if it didn't work. To switch metaphors, most people in the sixteenth and seventeenth centuries viewed abolishing the enforcement of a shared religion in roughly the same way we would view abolishing the fire department and leaving each household in charge of putting out its own fires. We have fire departments because a fire in one house isn't just a danger to that house, it's a danger to the whole community – and it's not feasible for each household to put out its own fires. Abolishing the fire department would be a terrible risk. Similarly, giving up on a shared community religion was risking a social catastrophe. The only thing that made the idea seem plausible was when people realized that enforced religious orthodoxy was undermining the moral order more than it was supporting it. The community's religious "fire departments" had become the leading cause of fires.

v. SOMETHING OLD, SOMETHING NEW

Locke organized his new reconciliation of religion and politics from a mixture of old and new elements. The most important of the "old" elements – that is, elements carried over from classical Greco-Roman philosophy and medieval Christian theology – included:

- Politics is primarily based on a transcendent moral law that governs right and wrong modes of social interaction. This transcendent moral law is known as the "natural law." The political order of a community exists to enforce this law.
- This natural law is known by all people, or at least it could potentially be known by all people (if anyone doesn't know it, that's only because he refuses to see it).
- Human nature is constructed in accordance with the natural law, such that people are generally happier and better off in the long run if they obey it.

- Because human nature is constructed in accordance with it, the influence of the natural law is visible in human behavior, and thus it is possible to determine much (though not necessarily all) of the content of the natural law by studying that behavior.
- There has been broad agreement across all civilizations in all times on the basic content of the natural law (e.g. don't kill, don't steal, keep your promises, help your neighbors). This broad agreement occurs because the natural law is visible to all and human nature is constructed in accordance with it.
- Although the political order of the community exists to enforce the natural law, the political order is not itself natural. It is artificial, and is established not by the rulers but by the whole community – because if the members of the community didn't uphold the political order, it would vanish. In this sense, the political order is created by the "consent" of the community. (This concept of "consent" has nothing to do with democracy; in this conception, monarchies are created by consent in the same way as democracies.)
- Although God commands that communities should create political institutions to enforce the natural law, God does not ordain what particular institutions the community should create. He instead commands people to use their reason and conscience to figure out for themselves what would be the best political order for the specific communities they live in. It is therefore legitimate for different societies in different circumstances to have different types of political orders.
- Because politics is primarily about enforcing right and wrong modes of social interaction, it is not an ultimate source of transcendent meaning or purpose and should not be a highly important part of human life in general.
- In particular, because politics is not an ultimate source of transcendent meaning, religion and politics each have a sphere of sovereignty that is autonomous from the other. Religious belief is not an excuse for disobeying legitimate civil laws – you cannot get a license to steal by saying that theft is part of your religion. On the other hand, the political order has no authority over religious beliefs or institutions (beyond the enforcement of legitimate civil laws).
- Religion and politics are both natural and necessary parts of human life. Both are essential to the survival of society, and each is essential to the survival of the other.

- Because the political order exists to enforce the natural law, if the rulers deliberately and consistently break the natural law, ruling for their own profit instead of for the good of the community, the community has the right to remove them – by force if necessary.

Some of these premodern elements were uncontroversial in Locke's time (e.g. politics is based on a transcendent moral law) and some of them had become highly controversial (e.g. the moral law is visible in human behavior). But all of these elements had long and venerable histories in western political philosophy and in Christian theology. All of them were central elements in medieval political and religious thought, and all of them were usually upheld as the majority view among medieval thinkers.

Alongside these premodern elements in Locke's thought was a strong strain of new thinking, characteristic of the period we now call "the Enlightenment," at least in the particular form it took in late seventeenth-century England. ("The Enlightenment" took dramatically different forms in different times and places.) The most important of these new elements influencing Locke's thought included:

- Tradition is not a source of authority. A tradition can be beneficial (as a teaching tool, as a source of moral inspiration, etc.) for those who willingly accept it. But people also have a right to reject traditions they disagree with, so appeals to tradition are not a legitimate way of settling disputes.
- Religious experience (as distinct from the Bible) also is not a source of authority.
- The Bible, on the other hand, is a source of authority, because it is God's word and people do not have a right to reject it – but its authority is spiritual, not coercive. God calls upon all people to obey the Bible, but he does not want anyone to use force to coerce people into obeying the Bible. The Bible itself says so. Thus, it is not legitimate for the political order to appeal to the Bible to justify its actions, or for anyone to use force in matters of religion generally. When people disobey the Bible, this is a matter for the church rather than the state, and the church must address it spiritually rather than coercively.
- Therefore, the political order may *only* enforce the natural law. Enforcing the natural law is not only government's main job, it

is its only job – it's not allowed to do anything else. In particular, it may not enforce any tradition or religious teaching. Every individual should be free to obey his or her own conscience. (Enforcing the natural law does not violate this freedom of conscience, because the natural law is visible to all so we know with certainty that everyone's conscience affirms it.)

- It follows that the community should not expect to have a social consensus on matters of religion, although it ought to maintain a social consensus on the natural law.
- Because of the increased distance of religion and politics under this way of thinking, politics is even more marginal to the central meaning of human life than medieval thought had understood.

These "new" elements were not new in the sense of being historically unprecedented. Each of these ideas had important precedents in earlier thought. What was new during the Enlightenment was the new way these ideas were combining and developing. While these ideas had all existed separately in various forms, the Enlightenment built them into a coherent structure and gave them new importance.

This larger dynamic played out in microcosm in Locke's own mind. Few of the important ideas in Locke's thought were original to Locke personally. He borrowed ideas extensively from other thinkers of his time. Locke's transformative contribution was not any particular new idea, but rather the new way he put ideas together. He combined ideas in new ways and drew them out to their logical conclusions more rigorously than others had.

Perhaps the most important aspect of this contribution was his intellectual ecumenicity. He drew individual ideas together from across a variety of different religious traditions and intellectual schools of thought and assembled them in a coherent and compelling way. At a time when the religious and intellectual world was increasingly fragmented and people of different beliefs and traditions were not effectively communicating with each other, that was an impressive achievement.

And Locke articulated these ideas in a way that was appealing to people across religious and intellectual barriers. Because his thought is so extensively indebted to so many different schools and traditions, he is not especially indebted to any one of them. His major works are not distinctively Anglican or Dissenting, Calvinist or Arminian, Latitudinarian or Puritan (to name a few of the key religious divisions of the day). They had a wide appeal and drew support from people of all points of view. Even where Locke does feel he has to take sides for one school of thought against another, he works to minimize his divisiveness and maximize the breadth of his appeal.[9]

vi. LOCKE AND MODERNITY

As we have already noted, Locke was not the only person to help shape this new reconciliation between religion and politics we call "modernity." And although he had some influence throughout the western world, he was not equally influential everywhere. Even in the English-speaking world, where his influence was by far the greatest, he was still only one (though the most important one) of a large number of influential figures.

Moreover, after Locke's time modernity developed in other directions that Locke and his contemporaries didn't foresee. That much is clear just from looking at the elements listed above – obviously many of the major components of "modernity" have changed dramatically since it first emerged. Some of these changes were further elaborations, extensions, or applications of elements that had always been implicit in Locke's thought. Others went directly against Locke's thinking and represented a clear break from his influence. And still others represented encounters with new problems and situations so radically different from anything Locke could have anticipated that it's hard to say anything about their relationship to Locke's thought one way or the other. We will look at these later developments in the concluding chapter.

But none of this detracts from the central and indispensable role Locke played in the emergence of religious freedom as the new mode of accommodation between religion and politics, and in turn the central and indispensable role religious freedom played in defining the modern world. Over the course of the book, we will see time and again how Locke's unique blending of classical, medieval, and Enlightenment ideas into a coherent intellectual structure gave shape to the world, and the worldview, that we inhabit today.

CHAPTER 1

LOCKE'S TIMES

From the beginning of his life to the peak of his career, Locke's social world was dominated by religious conflict. As a child he grew up in the midst of the English Civil War, which was especially hideous even by the standards of religious wars. And he reached the height of his political and philosophical achievements during the Glorious Revolution, when a despotic king was forcibly deposed and the autonomy of Parliament was formally recognized for the first time in England's history.

The entire period in between was one long, slow-motion political crisis, all driven by the same underlying religious conflict. Assassinations were periodically attempted. Criminal trials were rigged with faked evidence and stacked juries. Conspiracies and counter-conspiracies were rampant. Powerful lords and ministers sponsored personal networks of spies to keep tabs on each other. At one point Parliament tried to block the king's successor from taking the throne, and the king responded by trying to abolish Parliament. A few years later, a full-scale rebellion was forcibly put down.

Yet after all this, Locke was able to live his last years in a stable society characterized by peace and relatively broad toleration. The Glorious Revolution of 1688 turned out to be the final convulsion of England's great century-and-a-half long political crisis over religion. And the reason it was final was because it achieved a new reconciliation of religion and politics – one designed and implemented by Locke's political allies and with his active partici-pation, and to which Locke's writings gave eloquent and influential expression.

i. THE CHURCH, THE STATE, AND THE
CONSCIENCE – THE REFORMATION

For about 1,500 years, from the first massive spreading of Christian belief in the third and fourth centuries until the later stages of the Enlightenment in the eighteenth century, Christianity provided the moral foundation of social order in Europe. That is, Christianity was the guiding framework that shaped people's concept of what was or was not legitimate. And for almost all of that time they looked to the church as the authoritative voice of Christian doctrine. It wasn't this or that specific church they looked to, but simply "the church" – in light of Christ's command that believers seek unity with one another, there was only one church and there could only ever be one church. Even the great schism between Rome and the Eastern churches in the eleventh century did not alter this basic reality. If you lived in the west then your church acknowledged the authority of Rome, while if you lived in the east it did not; but wherever you were in the Christian world, if you wanted to know what was or was not consistent with Christian doctrine, the authoritative answer would come from "the church."

Throughout the history of Christianity, the nature and extent of church authority had been widely debated. Everyone acknowledged that it was the job of civil rulers, not the clergy, to rule the political community. But they also thought the church had the right to say what kind of behavior was and was not morally acceptable – even by the rulers. This implied a need for some sort of division of authority between the civil rulers and the clergy. Exactly how to draw the boundary between the two, and who should settle disputes over that boundary when they arose, was a subject of endless debate. It was not uncommon for civil rulers to ignore church dictates when they felt the church was overstepping its bounds. But the underlying assumption that "the church" was the final judge of theological questions and therefore had to share some measure of authority over social life was not disputed.[10]

These premises could no longer be taken for granted after Martin Luther raised his challenge to the traditional notion of church authority in the early 1500s. Luther succeeded, where a long line of previous would-be reformers had failed, in persuading millions of Europeans that "the church" did not have final and ultimate authority to declare what was or was not Christian doctrine. It was instead the responsibility of every individual believer to learn Christian doctrine from scripture for himself. The church was needed to help people do this, by teaching and exhorting, but the ultimate right and duty of discerning truth from error lay with the individual. As he wrote, "every man is responsible for his own faith."[11]

Since the medieval view of church authority had been woven into the fabric of the political and social order for more than a thousand years, everywhere Protestantism spread, political turmoil followed. By the 1550s, Protestants were either a majority or a very large minority in Germany, England, France, and the Netherlands as well as numerous smaller countries; the only major European powers with no large Protestant movements were Spain and Portugal. Almost every political system on the continent was thrown into chaos.[12]

The sixteenth-century Reformation did not much challenge the view that Christianity should provide the moral basis of politics and society. For the most part, it still wanted government to look to Christianity for a standard of right and wrong to guide its behavior. It only challenged the view that the church was the authoritative judge of what Christianity teaches.[13]

As a result, while the medieval view of church authority was supplanted in places where Protestants were in power, this did not result in the removal of Christianity from the political order. Rather, a different understanding of Christianity and different views of who had the authority to resolve theological disputes became the basis of the social order in these places. Protestants, who shared a broad agreement with one another on the fundamentals of theology, disagreed extensively on how to settle theological disputes.

A variety of approaches were tried in different countries. In Germany, starting in 1555 the emperor allowed the local ruler of each town to decide for himself what theology would guide his rule, and to appoint the local priest. From 1598 to 1685, the king of France extended a similar, but much more limited, form of religious autonomy to local rulers who had converted to Protestantism. In Scotland and Geneva, by contrast, civil rulers were expected to defer to church "elders" on theological questions, and the elders were in turn elected by the whole population.

These approaches had intermittent success in relieving the problem of religious violence – but only intermittent success. Even at the end of the seventeenth century, wars of religion and political chaos continued to rock the nations of Europe. One scholar sums up the reality on the ground concisely:

> The seventeenth century has often been called the age of reason and genius. ... But this spirited picture is only one face of that remarkable century. For the vast majority of the men and women who lived in Europe during Locke's century, the immediate reality was very different. It was a time of violence, death, rape, war, and devastation on a vast scale. It was years of religious strife caused by sectarian disputes over the right reading of scriptures and the flaunting of royal despotism justified by the doctrine of the divine right of kings. It was a world of constant religious and political intolerance and repression, and of ensuing dislocation that made fugitives wander across the lands of Europe in search of peace and security.[14]

ii. FROM BAD TO WORSE – THE ENGLISH REFORMATION

The situation in England, however, was unique. During his break from Rome, Henry VIII had taken direct control of the church throughout England, creating the new Church of England (or "Anglican" church). He had used this power aggressively to root out his opponents, impose universal edicts on church doctrine and practice, and (not incidentally) seize large amounts of church lands and wealth for himself.

His successors on the throne continued to make use of these powers. While it was generally understood that Henry had been a greedy and power-hungry man, the monarchs who followed him (both Protestant and Catholic) maintained the centralization of church control he had created. The function of authority – both political and religious – is to settle disputes, so naturally there should not be two authorities in society, competing with one another. Who would resolve the conflicts between them? Religious and political authority had to be in agreement with one another if either one were to function rightly.

The religious struggle was therefore nationalized in England to a far greater extent than it had been anywhere else. Indeed, "the religious struggle in England" had been so thoroughly centralized that at any given moment, all religious issues really came down to only one question: Which people or policies currently have the favor of whoever happens to be on the throne?

Although this centralization of power was justified as a way to end social conflict by having a single authority, in fact it only transferred the arena of conflict. Competing nobles and ministers with different religious preferences jockeyed with one another for the monarch's favor. Those who were "out" fought furiously to topple (or assassinate) those who were "in," while those who were "in," fearing to be displaced, encouraged the monarch to suppress and persecute their opponents who were "out."

And since a change of monarchs meant a change of religious authority, the line of succession was also a constant source of conflict. When – as repeatedly happened – the successor was of a different religious affiliation from the current monarch, those who shared the successor's preferences would attempt to assassinate the monarch, while those who shared the monarch's preferences would attempt to assassinate the successor.

Political loyalty and religious belief became intertwined. Because the church was directly under the monarch's control, dissent from the church was a sign of political disloyalty. And the supreme disloyalty was to be Roman Catholic under a Protestant monarch, or Protestant under a Catholic one.

All these problems were dramatically intensified – in a way that would continue to reverberate in English politics for centuries – in 1570. In that year, the pope issued a bull declaring that English subjects did not have to obey Queen Elizabeth, or acknowledge her government, because she was a heretic. This strongly reinforced the Protestant perception that adherence to Roman Catholicism was a form of civil treason. The Vatican declared the bull unenforceable (because it could not be publicly distributed in England) in 1580, essentially rendering it void. But the damage had been done; Protestant Englishmen would continue to view Catholicism as treasonous for long afterward.

Moreover, the centralization of religious authority in England actually created a new kind of political and religious conflict. Although "dissenting" churches did exist, the government strongly discouraged them and limited the rights of those who worshipped in them. Everyone across the religious spectrum was supposed to worship together in one national church.

Because of this expectation, the national church found it expedient to water down or compromise its doctrine and practice on controversial points wherever possible. On any question where the monarch did not demand a particular position, it was best for the church to take no clear position at all. Even those positions the monarch had ordered the church to take had a tendency to get watered down or compromised away over time. That way it was easier for people with a variety of different religious preferences to swallow their various disagreements and all show up for worship at the same national church.

Not surprisingly, there was a substantial movement reacting against this theological ambiguity. Adherents of this movement were called "Puritans" because they sought to purify the church of ambiguity and compromise. They pressed for England to adopt a clear and unambiguous commitment to the "Reformed" school of theology, which had been influential on the Church of England's founders and had already prevailed in the Church of Scotland. The church has no purpose, the Puritans argued, unless it has a clear teaching. They also hoped that establishing precise, comprehensive standards for doctrine and worship would give the church more autonomy from the ever-changing whims of the throne – a point that was not lost on the monarchs, who saw Puritanism as a threat to their influence. Some of the Puritans were inside the Church of England, struggling to reform it from within; others worshiped separately, in Presbyterian or other dissenting churches, hoping the nation would gradually come to prefer their model to the Church of England's.

Thus, instead of the twofold religious conflict prevailing in most of Europe, England had managed to create a threefold religious conflict. On one side were the Roman Catholics, constantly struggling to restore the Church of England to Roman control, or failing that, secure the right to worship in their own churches without giving up their civil rights. On the other side were the Puritans, struggling to establish a Reformed church in England on the model of Scotland and Geneva, or failing that, secure the right to worship in the Reformed manner (within the Church of England or outside it) without giving up their civil rights. In the middle were the conservative Anglicans – doctrinally ambiguous but firmly monarchistic, willing to compromise extensively on what was said and done within the national church but sternly insisting that no one ought to worship outside it.

iii.   DEEP DIVISION – OR, PLAYING GAMES WITH GOD'S LAW

The depth of these tensions is illustrated by a national crisis sparked by events in Locke's own hometown in 1632, the year of his birth. A local controversy had been brewing in Wrighton for some time over the practice of playing sports on Sunday. Some of the people of Wrighton liked to play a game called "fives" in the church yard. The game was rough enough that it led not only to broken windows but even to damaged walls. However, the churchwardens were much more offended by the fact that it was played on the Lord's Day, which Christians are commanded to "keep holy."

The Wrighton churchwardens, and many of the people of Wrighton, were Puritans. Like most English Puritans they believed recreation on the Lord's Day was forbidden by God. But the Church of England had not adopted this view, and for generations the non-Puritan population of Wrighton had enjoyed the right to play sports (and hold dances and "ales") on Sunday.

The local rector, Samuel Crook, was firmly Puritanical and had grown very popular with the people of Wrighton over his 30 years of service. He had struggled for years to impose stricter Sunday restrictions in Wrighton. However, his superior, Bishop William Piers, was firmly anti-Puritan and overruled Crook whenever he could. But Crook's local popularity limited Piers' ability to constrain him, and they wrangled back and forth for years.

Frustrated by the bishop's obstruction of their rector, a group of Puritan congregants persuaded a local panel of judges to impose tighter Sunday restrictions by civil law. They argued that Sunday recreation was not only bad for religious reasons but also had a negative impact on civil concerns, so it was proper for civil judges to rule on the matter. Bishop Piers was livid – not only at the institution of a Sunday policy he disagreed with, but at the civil government's interference with what had traditionally been the church's authority to determine Sunday regulations.

Bishop Piers brought the case to the new Archbishop of Canterbury, William Laud, who was even more anti-Puritan than Piers. Laud demanded that the judges' order be overruled, and the king, Charles I, sided with him. Charles wrote a declaration endorsing Sunday recreation and ordered every church in the whole English nation to read it during Sunday services. He also reissued a book his father had written in favor of sports on Sunday, occasioned by a similar controversy, and recommended it particularly to the people of Somerset – where Wrighton was located.

For those who favored the traditional Anglican view, it was a reassuring victory against a power grab by the forces of religious radicalism and dangerous innovation. For Puritans, it was not only a violation of the Lord's Day but a power grab by an overbearing monarch who didn't seem to take God's law seriously and wasn't willing to let them do things their own way in their own local churches and communities.

A few people playing a simple game in the Wrighton churchyard had shaken the whole country. "The ... crisis divided mortally not only Somerset, but England," writes one historian. "Men who loved their church and their traditions were strengthened in their loyalty to their king and bishops; the Puritans' hostility to both was hardened. The compulsory reading of the declaration brought war appreciably nearer."[15]

Now take the potential to produce that kind of destructive impact and multiply it by every single local controversy over a religious question anywhere in England, and the scale of the religious problem in seventeenth-century English politics becomes clear.

iv. THE CIVIL WAR AND ITS AFTERMATH

Over time, the Puritan cause had come to be identified with Parliament. This was partly because the conservative Anglicans were so closely associated with the monarchy. It was only natural that the Puritans would seek support in a sphere outside the king's immediate control. And it was also only natural that Parliament – which competed against the king for power and influence – should be attracted to a religious cause that would reduce the king's control of the church.

The English Civil War broke out between factions loyal to Charles and Parliament in 1642. The specific controversies that gave rise to the Civil War are numerous and complex, but the primary underlying reason Charles and Parliament found it impossible to settle their differences peacefully was the overwhelming distrust created by the religious rivalry between the heavily Puritan Parliament and the conservative Anglican monarchy.

Locke was ten years old when the war broke out. His father served as the captain of a cavalry regiment on Parliament's side. However, it is unclear whether or how his family's allegiance with the Puritans in Parliament rubbed off on him. The adult Locke did favor parliamentary autonomy and feared the encroachments of the king's power, but he also strongly favored the tradition of doctrinal ambiguity and pragmatic flexibility within the Church of England, rejecting the Puritans' preference for doctrinal clarity and uniformity. And he had a decidedly negative view of "dissenters" who worshiped outside the national church, including Puritans, tending to view them as inflexible and fanatical.[16] So the influence of his family's allegiances is ambiguous. The only thing we can really say with certainty about the influence of his childhood experience of the war is that it persuaded him that violent religious conflict is an ever-present danger in society and that rulers should make preventing it a high priority.

The war raged on and off for ten years, with the last convulsions coming to a halt in 1652. During this period Charles was captured and eventually executed, and the parliamentarians set up a republic and established a Puritan national church. But the republic proved unstable and it ultimately lasted for less than a decade after the end of the war, falling apart shortly after the death of its leader, Oliver Cromwell, in 1658. Two years later, order was restored through a settlement between the parliamentary and monarchist factions; the settlement restored the monarchy by putting Charles I's son and heir on the throne as Charles II.

This settlement restored peace, for the moment, but it did not restore trust. The great threefold religious conflict between Roman Catholic, conservative Anglican and Puritan Englishmen had been brought to a state of truce but it had not been settled. For a long time afterward, it was widely feared that the truce might break down and violence might return at any time.

v. AT OXFORD – LOCKE THE AUTHORITARIAN

The young adult Locke was immersed in this ongoing conflict while on the faculty of Oxford University. Like all important institutions in England during this period, Oxford was the subject of power struggles as the different factions sought to gain power and influence. Proving your loyalty to the right faction – which at Oxford meant proving your loyalty to the king and his church – was as much a part of getting ahead as scholarly merit. At one point, following a visit to Oxford from the king, the chancellor of the university was left feeling he had no choice but to purge those whose loyalty was in question; he reluctantly eased them out as gently as he could.[17]

Fortunately for Locke, his sincere preference for traditional Anglicanism and a strong monarchy was clear to all. While on the Oxford faculty, Locke wrote a series of tracts on the authority of government. Clearly shaped by Locke's fear of religious conflict, the tracts advocate absolute government authority as the only way to prevent the development of dissenting, fanatical movements in society. With a strong and assertive government – which in practice meant a strong king and a weakened Parliament – ensuring that everyone believes and behaves in basically the same way, there would be no room for the division and conflict that causes societies to break down.

The tracts particularly recommend government-enforced uniformity in matters of religion, keeping everyone obedient to the official religious position of the nation – though in the context of the traditional Anglican commitment to compromise and flexibility within the national church. This was the only way to prevent the growth of rival churches, which were the engines – or so Locke thought at the time – of religious conflict.

Yet Locke did not follow the traditional path of Oxford faculty, which was to join the clergy of the Church of England. Although no one questioned his loyalty to the church, taking orders as a clergyman would still have enhanced his career prospects.[18] But Locke had developed other intellectual interests that drew him to other pursuits.

During his studies, Locke had disliked the abstract and systematic approaches that dominated the study of theology and philosophy. He hated having to study the medieval "scholastic" theologians; later, he would equally dislike overly rationalistic Enlightenment philosophers like Descartes.[19] What he disliked in both was what he saw as their rigid insistence on dogmatic systems and their hubristic attempt to use abstract reasoning to develop answers to the great mysteries of the universe. As we will see in Chapter 2, Locke would later blame both these ideological tendencies – the traditionalism embodied in the medieval scholastics and the rationalism embodied in the radical Enlightenment – as important causes of religious conflict in society, alongside the problem of religious fanaticism.

But Locke embraced with great excitement intellectual movements that were geared toward the concrete rather than the abstract. He became fascinated with the emerging approach to natural science that relied on experimentation and empirical investigation; he read extensively from the stream of new books written by explorers and travelers, giving accounts of what the world was like beyond Europe – especially in the "new world" of the Americas; and he read deeply in classical Greco-Roman ethical and political philosophy, especially in Cicero, which focused on finding practical approaches to managing real-world dilemmas.

He ultimately settled on medicine, one of the most practical of all academic disciplines, as his field of specialty. No doubt one reason for this decision was the asthma and other chronic ailments that plagued Locke throughout his life; health was an issue of immediate concern for him. But it was also a choice consummately suited to his very practically oriented mind and temperament.

vi. IN CLEVES – AUTHORITARIANISM CHALLENGED

Locke's comfortable confidence in the wisdom of maintaining social order by squashing dissent was shaken by a series of experiences in his own life. One particular event, which may or may not have been the most important (such things are hard to judge) but was certainly the most dramatic, was a trip outside of England.

Considering diplomacy as a possible career path, in 1665 Locke signed up to serve as secretary to an important English diplomatic mission to Germany. England was at war with the Dutch over trade, and it badly wanted the elector of Brandenburg to become its ally, or at least remain neutral. The mission turned out to require surprisingly little work – the elector cut through all the niceties by simply telling them that his loyalty was for sale, and England was welcome to try to buy it – so Locke was left with plenty of time on his hands.

He used it to explore the city of Cleves, where he was staying with the mission. Although Cleves was located in northwestern Germany, it was legally part of the Electorate of Brandenburg – located in the east – due to a quirk of hereditary succession. In the decentralized political system of Germany, such arrangements were not unusual. But in the case of Cleves it had produced something that made a deep impression on Locke.

The elector had instituted a policy of religious toleration in Cleves. Germany was deeply divided over religion, and religious tensions were a part of life there – Locke reported in letters home that the people of Cleves feared that war might break out between Protestant and Roman Catholic princes. But unlike England, Germany had long since given up trying to force all its people to join a single church; each local prince was given control over religious policy in his own domains. In Cleves, the elector of Brandenburg permitted a wide variety of churches – Lutheran, Calvinist, Roman Catholic and others – and each person could worship as he chose. Even those few religious laws that were on the books were not enforced; Locke noted in a letter home that Quaker services were forbidden but that the Quakers of Cleves "take no notice" of the prohibition.[20]

By the philosophy Locke held at Oxford, Cleves should have been falling apart. With so many different churches, they should all have been constantly wrestling for predominance over the community – and hence the power to shape the civil laws. Each church should have been denouncing the laws (and rulers) it disagreed with as illegitimate and at enmity with God. A descent into chaos and anarchy should have already begun.

Yet none of this was happening. In fact, the opposite was happening. There was no political conflict over religion. Different churches each worshipped in their own ways, and it had no negative impact on civil relations at all. Most crucial of all, the adherents of the different churches *didn't even hate each other*. He wrote home to his friend and mentor, the great scientist Robert Boyle:

> They quietly permit one another to choose their way to heaven; and I cannot observe any quarrels or animosities amongst them on account of religion. This good correspondence is owing partly to the power of the magistrates, and partly to the prudence and good nature of the people, who, as I find out by inquiry, entertain different opinions without any secret hatred or rancor.[21]

The people of Cleves were worried that the princes of Germany were going to go to war with each other over God, but they themselves felt no inclination to do so.

Locke did note the role of "the power of the magistrates" in keeping the peace, resonating with his established belief in the importance of a powerful government. But the total absence of underlying religious tension in a society characterized by religious diversity clearly challenged the very roots of Locke's whole conception of the nature of religious conflict. Apparently a diversity of religious belief and practice need not cause, or be caused by, hostility between religious groups – and hence it need not be a civil danger.

While in Cleves, Locke attended worship services in a variety of churches – including Lutheran, Calvinist, and Roman Catholic ones – and roundly disliked them all. But while his Anglican religious preferences were reinforced by the experience, his authoritarian political preferences were undoubtedly challenged.

vii. LORD ASHLEY – AUTHORITARIANISM RENOUNCED

The diplomatic mission to Cleves ended in failure – the Elector's price was too high for England, and he sold out to the Dutch instead. But Locke's superiors were impressed with his performance and offered him more such work. Locke, however, decided against pursuing a diplomatic career and returned to Oxford.

One possible reason was personal. A noticeably handsome man, Locke had courted with a series of women at Oxford, and had exchanged flirtatious letters with at least one female correspondent (and possibly more) during his stay in Cleves.[22] A diplomatic career would have meant permanent separation from that circle of acquaintances.

But more prominent in his thoughts appears to have been his desire to return to science. He embarked on a series of more ambitious scientific researches, conducting experiments in the field and reading more deeply on the philosophy of science. For the first time he read the works of Descartes, the famous champion of the experimental method of science. In contrast to the more empirical approach he had learned from his mentor Boyle, Locke was appalled to discover that Descartes grounded the scientific method in a complex and (in Locke's opinion) highly speculative metaphysical philosophy. Locke read extensively in the critics of Descartes, and they deeply influenced his later writings on epistemology.[23]

It was at this time that Locke chose to embark on a career in medicine. And it was not long before this decision brought a decisive end to Locke's youthful authoritarianism – by leading him to meet the man whose friendship would transform him and define his adult life as a philosopher.

Shortly after returning to Oxford in 1666, Locke met Anthony Ashley Cooper. Ashley sought out Locke because he needed help coping with chronic health problems and Locke had been highly recommended to him as a physician. Ashley, then a baron, was sufficiently impressed with Locke to begin promoting his career. He pulled strings – even procuring a letter of support from the king – to help Locke secure a permanent position at Oxford where he could study medicine full time.

The following spring, Ashley persuaded Locke to move to London and join his household as his personal physician. In addition to his burgeoning friendship with Ashley, Locke was attracted to London because it was emerging as the epicenter of the new movement for empirical science. Living there and having Ashley's connections would open up a whole new world of possibilities in science for him.

But that was not the direction Locke's life actually took. London was first and foremost the center of the English political world, and Ashley was first and foremost a politician. And the particular shape of Ashley's politics forced Locke to confront politics in a dramatically new way.

Ashley's political career was defined by his longtime championing of two causes that, until recently, Locke had detested: religious toleration and the autonomy of Parliament against the king. During the Civil War, he had joined the parliamentary rebellion after he became convinced that the king was planning to stamp out religious freedom for Protestants. But during the republican period after the king was deposed, Ashley found himself under constant suspicion by the Puritan leadership because his religious preferences didn't line up perfectly with theirs, and he became a voice for religious toleration in the republic. As the republic was collapsing, he was one of a group of moderate parliamentarians who urged compromise with the royalists and eventually negotiated the settlement that brought the king back to power.

Perhaps most important, Ashley's interest in religious toleration was motivated primarily by the same consideration that had driven Locke to oppose it: a desire for civil peace. Locke had opposed toleration because he wanted to defuse political conflict over religion. Ashley supported toleration to accomplish precisely the same result.

Ashley's influence was therefore just what was needed to transform Locke into a champion of toleration. And Locke was brought into Ashley's orbit just after his trip to Cleves had given him a powerful object lesson on the value of toleration.[24]

In 1667, the same year he accepted Ashley's invitation to London, Locke poured considerable time and effort into producing an essay defending religious toleration. Before long, Ashley had made Locke one of his political advisors. Locke began meeting the powerful lords and politicians of Ashley's circle, who were impressed by his combination of powerful intellect and personal modesty. Locke became a regular participant in the private conversations through which Ashley and his allies shaped their goals, strategy, and tactics.

The following year, Locke saved Ashley's life by overseeing a daring surgical operation. A silver tube was inserted into Ashley's abdomen, through which fluid would be drained three times a day for four months. Removing the tube was deemed too dangerous, so Ashley carried it around for the rest of his life – a constant reminder of his friendship with the young doctor he had discovered at Oxford.

But medicine and science moved to the background of Locke's career. Even though he owed his life to Locke's medical genius, Ashley began discouraging Locke from spending any of his time on medicine. He wanted Locke to devote his time to the philosophical study of politics, religion, and economics. For all Locke's scientific potential, Ashley saw Locke's potential to do even greater things by devoting his life to the cause of freedom.

With Ashley's encouragement, Locke began composing longer and more serious writings on the deeper theological and philosophical issues involved in the debate over religious toleration. He had retreated from these subjects at Oxford – especially from the more technical branches of philosophy like epistemology, the study of knowledge – because of their abstraction and irrelevance to practical matters. But in his debates and discussions, he had found that he couldn't make the most full and forceful case for toleration without raising issues that required a technical theological and philosophical treatment. Locke doggedly struggled with these intellectual issues throughout the 1670s and 1680s. His largest undertaking was a book on epistemology that focused on the issues raised by religious and political problems. When finally published in 1689, the *Essay Concerning Human Understanding* had reached over 700 pages and became one of the landmark works in the history of epistemology, earning Locke international fame.

viii. A NEW STORM GATHERS

The year 1667 had been one of the more eventful in Ashley's extraordinarily eventful life. In addition to Locke's fateful move to London, Ashley rose to much greater political prominence. After England suffered a disastrous loss in its war with the Dutch, the Lord Chancellor took the blame and was driven from office. In the bureaucratic reorganization that followed, Ashley became one of a group of five government ministers who between them consolidated a great deal of the power that was not directly in the king's hands.

The group was called "the cabal," a name derived from the initials of its five members. The meaning we now give to this word – a dangerous conspiracy consisting of a few powerful people – suggests how much power Ashley and his partners possessed. It especially reflects the perception of the king and his allies, who saw Ashley's group as power-hungry and potentially treacherous; to them, the cabal's existence represented a critical threat to the rights and proper authority of the king. For their part, the parliamentarians viewed the king in much the same way.

It is not surprising, then, that Ashley worked so insistently to develop Locke's potential as a political advisor. In the emerging power struggle between Parliament and the king, Ashley needed all the help he could get.

In the years that followed, the power struggle only intensified, and Ashley became one of the foremost critics of the king's desire to expand his power. Convinced that the king was conspiring to roll back traditional English liberties, Ashley maintained a network of spies and informants to keep tabs on the king's activities.

In 1672, the cabal split up due to internal feuding. Ashley, always a shrewd political operator, managed to avoid getting entangled in the conflict. After several of his colleagues were driven from office, he temporarily rose to the position of Lord Chancellor and was elevated from baron to earl, becoming the first Earl of Shaftesbury. Though he left the Lord Chancellor's office in 1673, he had positioned himself as the foremost political opponent of the king and his allies.

At about this time – we don't know exactly when – Ashley discovered that his suspicion of the king had been well founded. His network of spies discovered that in 1670, seeking help in the war against the Dutch, Charles had made a promise to the king of

France that he would – someday, when the time was right – publicly convert to Roman Catholicism and return England to Roman Catholic religious control.[25]

Today, with the benefit of hindsight, we may question how important this promise really was. Charles did not commit to a timetable for fulfilling his promise to return England to Roman Catholicism, and he reigned for another 15 years without ever moving toward fulfilling it.

But at the time, Ashley and his circle had no way of knowing whether the king intended to fulfill the promise. The mere fact that the promise had been made redoubled all of their suspicions about his ambitions. They felt that their freedom to worship as Protestants was in danger – and that if England ceased to be a Protestant power, the very existence of Protestantism itself, anywhere in the world, might be endangered.[26]

This escalating power struggle between the king and Parliament over religious toleration helped move Locke further into alignment with Ashley's political views. At Oxford, Locke had not only been authoritarian in religious matters, but in the rivalry between Parliament and the king he had been a firm royalist. Now, having already converted to the view that religious toleration was the path to civil peace and religious authoritarianism the path to conflict, Locke came to see the king as an immanent threat to religious freedom – and hence to civil peace. Locke became as much an advocate of Parliament as he had been an advocate of the king at Oxford.

ix. THE STORM BREAKS – THE EXCLUSION CRISIS

The seething distrust between Parliament and the king, and between Puritans, traditional Anglicans and Roman Catholics, built up steadily through the 1670s. It finally exploded in a new crisis that threatened a return to the horrors of civil war.

Charles, having produced no legitimate children, had named his younger brother, the Duke of York, as his successor, rather than his illegitimate son, the Duke of Monmouth. York was Roman Catholic, and the prospect of his succession to the throne was widely anathema to Protestants. In 1678 public accusations were made that Catholic agents were conspiring to assassinate the king in order to put York, one of their own, on the throne. The accusations were later exposed as fraudulent, but they heightened anxieties among those fearful of Catholic rule.

Shaftesbury began a campaign to exclude James from the succession to the throne. In 1679 his allies in Parliament introduced the Exclusion Bill, which would have done precisely this. Charles, fearing that the House of Commons would pass the bill, exercised his power to dissolve Parliament for new elections. When a new Parliament was elected, Charles delayed it from starting its work as long as he could, and then when the Exclusion Bill and a series of other bills motivated by similar concerns were finally introduced, he dissolved Parliament again in 1681.

The king's determination not to allow the House of Commons to act against him took the fears of his opponents to a much higher level. One of the events that had led to the English Civil War a generation earlier had been Charles I's ill-fated attempt to rule all England alone, with no Parliament at all, believing that God had placed all rightful political authority in his hands.[27] As his son Charles II dissolved Parliament after Parliament to prevent the passage of legislation he opposed, Shaftesbury and his allies recalled what they had seen as the tyrannical ambitions of his father in the 1630s and concluded that the apple had not fallen far from the tree.

Parliament was not the only arena of conflict. Criminal trials were used as political weapons; accusations (true and false) of various crimes, accompanied by suborned testimony and faked evidence, were seen as a convenient way of eliminating key opposition figures.

Some abuses were committed by the king's opponents. In the notorious case known as the "Popish Plot," trumped-up allegations of an assassination supposedly being planned by a Roman Catholic conspiracy led to increased persecution and newly tightened legal constraints on the civil rights of Catholics. Shaftesbury harnessed this hysteria to rally support for the cause of limiting the king's powers – and to advance himself.[28]

But the king and his allies had far more power in their hands, and they used it. One historian summarizes the breadth and depth of the king's campaign to destroy his opponents:

> Kings not merely were able to rule without Parliament, or to control its composition by changing the franchise, but they also imprisoned, fined to the point of financial ruin, and executed political opponents who defended Englishmen's liberties, pamphleteers who propagandized on behalf of such liberties, printers

who published their pamphlets, authors whose manuscripts were seized during warrantless searches of their homes, and correspondents who wrote disparaging comments in private letters – which the executive opened as they were sent through the mail. The crown dismissed judges who opposed these measures as incursions on Englishmen's liberties. And Englishmen's right to trial by jury when faced with a treason charge was eviscerated, not merely by defendants in such trials not being allowed legal representation, nor a copy of the indictment, nor any right of appeal, but even more by [the executive's] ability to dismiss judges and pack juries, including by changing the electorate for officials who appointed juries, and [to] move trials to other locations in order to secure compliant judges and juries. ... The Crown [undertook] legal moves to remove its political opponents and religious dissenters from the franchise and juries of London, and forced [the] surrender of the civic constitution of London in a trial in which it removed judges and appointed as the presiding judge the lawyer who had drawn up the tenuous legal case against the city.[29]

Charles was giving his opponents plenty of reasons to view him as an aspiring tyrant.

Shaftesbury himself was put on trial for treason in 1681. The evidence against him was weak and he was acquitted, but shortly thereafter he did commit treason – in early 1682, Charles fell ill and Shaftesbury spearheaded a plot to lead an armed rebellion to prevent York's succession. Charles recovered, so the plot never came to fruition, but at this point it seemed clear that a new civil war was all but inevitable – England was already in something like a state of undeclared civil war.

It was during this crisis that labels "Whig" and "Tory" first appeared.[30] The formation of separate parties on what we would now call "liberal" and "conservative" lines, originally based on the question of whether constitutional sovereignty was shared between the king and Parliament or ultimately rested entirely in the king, was to define the parameters of politics in the English-speaking world from that time forward.

Later in 1682, supporters of the king won the elections for control of law enforcement offices in London, and Shaftesbury feared he could not survive another treason trial. He had also suffered repeated defeats in the struggle to pass legislation against the king – including not only the king's efforts to prevent the House of Commons from voting, but stiff opposition in the House of Lords. Shaftesbury fled the country to exile in Amsterdam, and died less than two months later, in January 1683.

Charles had won the battle of the Exclusion Crisis. But the war was far from over.

x. THE REVOLUTIONARY LOCKE

The Exclusion Crisis had a deeply radicalizing effect on the parliamentary opposition, and few were more dramatically radicalized than Locke. During this period, he composed a book defending the people's right to violent revolution against tyrants, *Two Treatises of Government*. "If the innocent, honest man must quietly quit all he has, for peace's sake, to him who will lay violent hands upon it," Locke writes, "I desire it may be considered, what a kind of peace there will be in the world, which consists only in violence and rapine, and which is to be maintained only for the benefit of robbers and oppressors" (T II.228, 231). And that's one of the book's more temperate lines.

The argument of the *Two Treatises* draws extensively from arguments being made by other Whigs during the Exclusion Crisis. Of particular importance is the 1681 book *Patriarcha non Monarcha* written by his friend James Tyrrell in response to the 1680 publication of an old manuscript, Robert Filmer's *Patriarcha*, arguing for absolute monarchy. A number of key arguments are shared between Tyrrell's book and Locke's, most importantly that all people are born free and equal; all government power is power transferred to it by individuals; the state of nature is not necessarily a war of all against all; there are five sharply distinct types of authority (parental, conjugal, political, master/servant, and lord/slave); and those who use power tyrannically forfeit their authority. While we cannot be absolutely sure of the sequence of events, it appears most likely that Locke read Tyrrell's book in between composition of the *First Treatise* and the *Second Treatise* and incorporated arguments borrowed from Tyrell into the *Second Treatise*.[31]

These arguments, in turn, grew out of a longer and older tradition. English Puritan political philosophy and theology had traced many of the same lines of argument during the Civil War period earlier in the century, and their influence is also a factor in Locke's argument.[32] And the approach to natural law, natural rights and the state of nature that were popular among Whigs in the 1680s can be traced back through a succession of medieval philosophers, all the way back to William of Ockham.[33]

Yet Locke's argument drove this philosophical framework in new directions. Tyrrell had limited his theory to a justification of revolution against out-of-control tyrants. Locke's theory implies a much more far-reaching commitment to limited government power over the individual.[34]

The book would not be published until years later, but it shows that before the end of the Exclusion Crisis Locke had become an advocate of political violence in the defense of civil liberties and the rights of the legislature. He had traveled the full length of the political spectrum from an authoritarian, royalist absolutist to a tolerationist, parliamentary revolutionary.[35]

xi.   IN AMSTERDAM – REBELLION CONTINUES

In 1683 Locke was forced to flee to the Netherlands, just like Shaftesbury and many other supporters of the Exclusion Bill. It must have been an extremely painful decision – among much else, he was in the throes of an emotionally tumultuous courtship with the daughter of a leading Cambridge Platonist, Damaris Cudworth, whom he had met the previous year. She seems to have wanted to accompany him to the Netherlands, but Locke opposed this. While the two remained close friends for the rest of their lives, Locke's exile had prevented a marriage; by the time he returned, she had married another man.[36]

In Amsterdam, Locke lived among a population of exiled English Whig refugees. Their revolutionary movement had not stopped with their exile from England.

In 1685, Charles died and his (Roman Catholic) brother the Duke of York ascended the throne as James II. The Duke of Monmouth, Charles's (Protestant) illegitimate son, staged a coup attempt with the assistance of the Whig exiles in the Netherlands. But the Monmouth Rebellion was quickly put down and Monmouth was captured and executed.

After the rebellion, James enlarged the army and appointed Catholics to command positions they had not previously been permitted to hold. At the same time, he dissolved Parliament for new elections and then refused to hold any new elections, setting up himself, alone, as the sole governing authority of England. The combination of these two events convinced his Protestant opponents all the more that James was an aspiring tyrant who would soon stamp out Protestantism for good.

It is not clear to what extent Locke was directly involved in helping craft the Monmouth Rebellion and other violent resistance efforts during his time in exile. He was, at minimum, a friend and supporter of those who did.

While in Amsterdam, Locke became increasingly interested in theology. Because the Netherlands had a policy of wide religious toleration and freedom of speech, it had become a refuge for people with unorthodox religious ideas. Amsterdam in the 1680s was a city of thriving religious debate and controversy. The most contentious debates centered on two questions that it was not legal to openly debate in most of Europe – the two questions that for two thousand years have provided the most commonly used definition of the boundary between orthodoxy and heresy for Christians: Is Jesus both God and a man? And is it his death and resurrection that saves sinners?

Locke had friends on both the orthodox and unorthodox sides of these debates, and was drawn into an extended study of them. Until this point he had been a solidly orthodox Anglican, but now he treated these two questions as open for reconsideration. His study continued, consuming an increasing portion of his time and attention, even after he later returned to England, and up through the final years of his life. History does not record what conclusions he reached.[37]

But there is one result of his theological struggles we do know: he became a deeply religious, rather than simply political, advocate of toleration. The issue of religious toleration not only stayed at the top of Locke's agenda, it found a new depth and passion as it became not simply an issue of politics, but of piety.

In the same year James took the throne in England, the king of France revoked that country's legal toleration for Protestants, which had stood for almost a century. France's large Protestant minority fled the country by the hundreds of thousands, many of them seeking refuge in the tolerant harbors of the Netherlands.

Between the failure of the Monmouth Rebellion (which Locke, as a Whig, viewed as a victory for tyranny) and the flood of French

Protestant refugees, the cause of religious freedom seemed to be worse off than ever. Locke responded by writing a new defense of toleration, this one less focused on political analysis than on the sheer cruelty and immorality of religious oppression. He wrote with a fiery anger and a depth of righteous indignation unmatched even when he was calling for violent revolution in the *Two Treatises*. "No man can be a Christian without charity, without that faith which works, not by force, but by love," he declares. "Now I appeal to the consciences of those that persecute, torment, destroy and kill other men upon pretense of religion, whether they do it out of friendship and kindness toward them or no?" (L 1, 14).

xii. THE GLORIOUS REVOLUTION AND LOCKE'S *ANNUS MIRABILIS*

During all these crises, one of James's most important political advantages was the fact that his daughter and heir, Mary, was a Protestant, and was married to an important Dutch Protestant prince, William of Orange. This tended to reduce the perception of James's rule as a threat to Protestants – he was a single Roman Catholic monarch who would serve his time and then be succeeded by a strongly Protestant couple.

But in 1688, James had a son. Since sons were favored over daughters in the succession, English Protestants were now facing the prospect of an intergenerational Catholic dynasty. There was no telling how long Catholics might sit on the throne.

This dramatically changed the game. Important Tory figures who had stood by James during the Exclusion Crisis and the Monmouth Rebellion were now willing to help the Whigs overthrow him. And since James's new heir meant that William of Orange would not be succeeding to the throne as expected, William – who had substantial military strength – became the leader of the English Protestant cause. The revocation of toleration for Protestants in France had also shifted international politics more favorably to the Whig cause. As he was preparing to invade England to depose James, William was prevailed upon by the Whigs to set a good example and demonstrate his commitment to toleration by intervening to prevent the exile of a religious dissenter in his own territories.[38]

In November 1688, William sailed from the Netherlands to England with a large navy carrying a large army. Just before the end of the year, James surrendered power, and in February 1689 William and Mary became the king and queen of England. Later that year, Parliament passed, and the king ratified, a piece of legislation called the Bill of Rights affirming Parliament's right to exist independent of the king and its control over taxation, and some basic personal liberties of Protestant citizens.

Locke returned to England in 1689 along with the exiled Whig community. In that year, his three most important works – the *Essay Concerning Human Understanding*, the *Letter Concerning Toleration*, and the *Two Treatises of Government* – the fruit of decades of long labor, were all finally published. As one Locke scholar has commented, 1689 was Locke's *annus mirabilis* – his year of wonders.[39]

For the remainder of his life, Locke held a series of civil service jobs in the new administration. He spent much time writing, and increasingly turned his attention to religion.

With the crisis over and religious tensions relieved, public discussion of religion turned to less immediately political matters. And with the greater legal tolerance instituted by the Whig regime, some religious issues that had previously been beyond discussion came under debate. Among other religious writings, Locke published a major book, *The Reasonableness of Christianity as Delivered in the Scriptures*, in 1695. His major goal was to lay out what he saw as the most fundamental elements of religious doctrine – to show that only a very basic understanding of doctrine was necessary to salvation. His goal was to persuade members of rival theological camps to accept each other as fellow Christians, on grounds that the basic doctrines required for salvation were things that they all agreed on. He also expressed a hope that the book would show deists and other rationalistic doubters that Christianity involved no unreasonable or irrational beliefs (hence the book's title). The book reflected the diverse influences Locke had picked up from his time in Amsterdam – from conservative Calvinists to liberal "Latitudinarians" to more radically unorthodox sources.[40]

xiii. LOCKE'S TIMES AND OURS

It should be obvious that Locke's times bear a number of similarities to our own. The fragmentation of society along religious lines is only the most obvious parallel. The fear that religious differences are fueling political conflict of various kinds, and may lead to far worse things, holds a prominent place in our public discourse.

Beyond the immediately religious divide, there is a broader lack of consensus about the framework of right and wrong within which laws and political action are conceived. People don't merely disagree about what priorities the government should set or what policies will be effective in achieving its goals. They approach politics with different ideas about what is fair and just, which is a far deeper division. In the United States, it is now common to hear people express doubts about whether people on the political and social right and people on the political and social left even have the same idea about what kind of country they live in.

The debate over government involvement in the real estate market in the context of the 2008 financial meltdown provides a clear example. One large part of the American population seems to think that "justice" or "fairness" requires the government to pressure banks to make loans to disadvantaged customers who would otherwise be deemed uncreditworthy. The other part seems to think that "justice" or "fairness" demands that the government not do this. What appears on the surface to be a difference of opinion about effective economic policy reveals itself, after only a little bit of investigation, to be a difference over the most fundamental basis of the entire political system – the standard of justice it applies.

The ideas of a seventeenth-century philosopher cannot be simply picked up out of his books and dropped immediately into the context of twenty-first-century politics. Much is different today. However, if a crisis like the one we face now has been faced before and effectively defused, we would be wise to go back and see how that was done. We cannot expect to learn everything we need to know, but we should expect to learn much that is valuable.

CHAPTER 2

LOCKE'S WORLDVIEW

In 1671, in Locke's personal rooms, he and a group of five or six friends were engaged in a frustrating discussion about morality and religion. The source of the discussion was a renewed public controversy over religious toleration touched off by a book arguing against it (Samuel Parker's *Discourse of Ecclesiastical Polity*) published the previous year.[41] The source of the frustration was that the group was struggling for answers the issues raised by the controversy, but couldn't make any headway. As Locke would later write in the introductory "epistle to the reader" in his *Essay Concerning Human Understanding*, they "found themselves quickly at a stand, by the difficulties that rose on every side" (E Epistle, 7).

At this point, Lord Ashley was nearing the top of his rise to power, and Locke had been a member of his political inner circle for several years. Religious toleration was no longer a matter of personal academic interest for Locke – his success or failure in making the case for toleration would have a real impact on whether English law would become more or less tolerant. Parker's book had produced political momentum for stricter religious laws, and stopping that momentum fell largely to Ashley. Thus, the intellectual job of refuting Parker fell largely to Locke. To be unable – after having thought and written about the subject, from both sides, for nearly a decade – to answer Parker's arguments satisfactorily when the stakes were so high must have been maddeningly frustrating.

Then Locke had a moment of inspiration – these intellectual problems could only be solved by going to a deeper philosophical level and wrestling with epistemology, the study of knowledge. "After we had a while puzzled ourselves," he relates, "without coming any nearer a resolution of those doubts which perplexed us, it came into my thoughts that we took a wrong course; and that, before we set ourselves on inquiries of that nature, it was necessary to examine our own abilities, and see what objects our understandings were, or were not, fitted to deal with." Locke's notes on Parker's book confirm that he thought he could only answer Parker's arguments by delving into the underlying epistemological issues.[42]

"This I proposed to the company," Locke writes of his idea for taking an epistemological turn, "who all readily assented; and thereupon it was agreed that this should be our first inquiry." Locke then decided to do something that must have seemed relatively minor at the time. "Some hasty and undigested thoughts, on a subject I had never before considered ... I set down against our next meeting" (E Epistle, 7).

Before the end of the year, those "hasty and undigested thoughts, on a subject I had never before considered" had become the draft of a book. Locke would labor continually to revise that book for 18 years until its publication as the *Essay* – and he would continue revising it, releasing a series of new and improved editions, continuing right up until his death.

The 700-page *Essay* was Locke's life's work. And while his political works have since become more famous, during his own life and for some time afterward it was the *Essay* for which Locke was primarily known. It was the only major work he published under his own name; his major political and religious works were all published under pseudonyms. And it remains to this day one of the most important books ever written on epistemology.

To give an overview of a book as lengthy as the *Essay* in one chapter is a daunting challenge. Locke's contributions on many topics in the *Essay* – such as the problems of free will and human responsibility or the question of what defines human personhood – we must leave aside for lack of space. Here we are only looking at those aspects of the *Essay* that directly relate to Locke's larger religious and political influence.

i. AN EPISTEMOLOGY OF RELIGION, MORALITY, AND POLITICS

Locke wasn't kidding when he wrote that epistemology was "a subject I had never before considered." While working on his master's degree he had despised the curriculum in medieval "scholastic" philosophy that he had been required to study.[43] Between obtaining

his master's in 1658 and that fateful day in 1671, he had read extensively in medicine, natural science, travel, theology and ethics, but
we have no record of his having read any significant amount on any
subject in technical philosophy.[44]

But Locke and his friends had discovered that it's cutting corners
to turn away from "abstract" technicalities and rush straight on to
"practical" problem-solving. That just lets you take for granted all
the assumptions and premises you use to solve practical problems,
instead of challenging your assumptions and learning how to justify
them – or else change them. If you don't go through that process,
then when someone like Samuel Parker comes along to challenge
your assumptions, you get a train wreck. Skipping over the technical stuff is short-circuiting the intellectual process; it's cheating.

This is a key difference between Locke's epistemology and that of
some other titanic figures in the history of the field. René Descartes
was driven to the study of knowledge because he had radical doubts
about whether it was really possible to know anything. In the most
famous story ever told about epistemology – actually, the only
famous story ever told about epistemology – we find him huddled
near a stove in a cold room, driven to distraction by the haunting
fear that his mind was systematically unsound. After all, if it were,
how would he know? How could he test it? Even to the simplest possible question – do I exist? – it seemed impossible to fully, ultimately
justify an answer. And then he realized that the very existence of the
question proved the existence of a questioner – "I think, therefore I
am." He had found one question to which he really knew the answer.
From this starting point he built his entire epistemology. Most other
famous epistemologists, although their stories are less dramatic
than Descartes', have also been fundamentally interested in the
question of whether the human mind is systematically sound or
unsound.

The *Essay* is completely unlike this. Locke has no interest in
investigating whether or not he exists and seems to regard the question as silly. "If anyone pretends to be so skeptical as to deny his
own existence (for really to doubt of it is manifestly impossible) let
him for me enjoy his beloved happiness of being nothing, until
hunger, or some other pain, convince him of the contrary" (E
IV.10.2, 619–620). And he is not really interested in most of the
other, similar questions regarded as basic by many epistemologists.
His treatment of how we can know there is an objective world that

exists outside our own minds is fairly superficial; he ends it by remarking that the certainty we have of the world's existence merely from "the testimony of our senses" is "not only as great as our frame can attain to, but as our condition needs" (E IV.11.8, 634). These issues are just not what the *Essay* is about; Locke is happy to simply assume that the mind works, and go from there.

What drives Locke is how to process the ideas that occur in the mind in a morally and socially responsible way. All around him he sees people dying, tortured, imprisoned, oppressed and suffering because of conflict over differences of belief. Clearly differences of belief are just about as gravely important a subject as there could be. So, since I am an individual who has beliefs, what are my responsibilities?

Thus Locke provides what you might call a "civic epistemology." It is an epistemology that doesn't so much probe the ultimate basis of knowledge as the need to process the knowledge we have responsibly. One scholar gave his book about the *Essay* the insightful title *John Locke and the Ethics of Belief*.[45] That hits the nail on the head – what drove Locke to spend most of his adult life on the *Essay* was the urgency of providing an ethics of belief.

ii. TRUTH – THE UNIVERSAL DESIRE

The essential problem confronting Locke was religious fragmentation. People with different beliefs didn't recognize the same rules, either for personal behavior or for structuring society. And since government exists to enforce such rules, this fragmentation produced political conflict. Each group wanted its rules, not the rules followed by other groups, to define public policy and constrain the behavior of its neighbors.

Groups with different beliefs could not simply ignore one another, because society needs to have at least some shared rules. To at least some extent, then, people with different beliefs need to be able to come together and agree on some rules.

What could bring people in mutually hostile belief groups together? Locke argues that, at bottom, what they share most fundamentally is a common desire to know the truth. "Nothing ... [is] so beautiful to the eye as truth is to the mind; nothing so deformed and irreconcilable to the understanding as a lie. For though many a man can with satisfaction enough own a no-very-handsome wife in his bosom, yet who is bold enough to openly avow that he has espoused a falsehood, and received into his breast so ugly a thing as a lie?" (E IV.3.20, 552).

The desire for truth is not abstract, intellectual, or academic. It is the universal wellspring of all that makes human life human rather than merely animal. The one thing everyone wants is to believe correctly and behave accordingly. Even the skeptic, who thinks that we cannot really know anything, believes that skepticism is in some sense the best belief system. Even the libertine or nihilist who rejects all behavioral rules beyond his own will thinks that this behavior is in some sense the best approach to life. And of course only a tiny number of people subscribe to these extreme views – most people manifest a strong commitment to believe what is *true* and do what is *right*.

In the *Essay*, Locke argues that people generally assume they already know, for the most part, what to think and how to behave. And because they value their beliefs, they teach them to their children (see E I.3.22, 81 and IV.7.11, 598–603). That's not wrong it itself; the problem is, they tend not to question what they've been taught, to see whether it's true (see E I.3.23, 82 and IV.20.9, 712). Thus, beliefs are perpetuated from parents to children through generation after generation without being sufficiently examined.

It is essential for every person to carry out a careful, diligent *search* for the truth that all of us desire and most of us think we already possess. "Nothing is so dangerous as principles … taken up without questioning or examination; especially if they be such as concern morality, which influence men's lives and give a bias to all their actions" (E IV.12.4, 642).

The great underlying themes of the *Essay* are the urgency and the sacredness of this search. "What is the truth, and am I following it?" is not a matter of ivory tower contemplation; it is the most practical of all questions. It is also the most noble – even the most holy.

Of course, we cannot diligently search for the truth on every possible question; the list of potential questions is endless. But we can search for truth on the most important questions – the ones that fundamentally define the meaning of human life. In particular, we have – almost by definition – a particular moral duty to examine the beliefs that shape our behavior. "Our business here is not to know all things, but those which concern our conduct," that is, to "find out those measures" by which a person "ought to govern his opinions and actions" (E I.1.6, 46).

To seek out the right views on those questions that "concern our conduct," and then frame our behavior accordingly, is something everyone can and must do. He writes of human beings that "how short soever their knowledge may come of a universal or perfect comprehension of whatsoever is, it yet secures their great concernments, that they have light enough to lead them to the knowledge of their maker, and the sight of their own duties" (E I.1.5, 45).

And even with all our less important beliefs, the ones we don't have time to investigate thoroughly, we must be open to such investigation in principle. You never know what might turn out to become important in the right set of circumstances, and if something becomes important you should be willing to test it. Perhaps there's no particular reason I need to check first whether the brakes in my car are working properly every single time I drive, but any time I see some specific indication that they might not be working, I had better test them before I get on the highway.

iii.   HOW THE TRUTH DIVIDES US

Of course, different people look for the truth in different places. The political problem begins when people who look for the truth in one place try to force what they believe on people who would prefer to look for the truth somewhere else. Thus the universal desire for truth is, on the surface, a source of conflict rather than a source of unity. Social conflict over belief arises precisely because everyone wants to know and follow the truth.

One place people seek truth is in traditions. Adherents of different traditions believe that their traditions have slowly collected truth over time and embodied them in what might be called an architecture of beliefs. A superstructure of beliefs crafted by thousands of people over centuries, goes the argument, is capable of containing more truth than any one person could scrape together in only one human lifetime using only one human being's mental powers.

Locke does not hold this view. He believes that on balance, traditions are more of a threat to the open investigation of knowledge than they are a help to gaining it. If they follow their traditions, "men have reason to be heathens in Japan, Mahumetans [i.e. Muslims] in Turkey, Papists in Spain, Protestants in England, and Lutherans in Sweden" (E IV.15.6, 657).

One thing that influenced his position on this point was the fierce academic debate that was going on in his time over natural science. Locke was an ardent follower of new Enlightenment approaches to natural science based on the experimental method, which the medieval traditions had rejected. Those traditions continued to keep Enlightenment approaches to science largely shut out of the major universities, much to Locke's frustration.[46]

But Locke's biggest argument is not with those who follow a tradition because they sincerely believe it contains truth. Much more important is his argument against those who divorce their traditions from a sincere search for truth – especially by trying to force their traditions on others against their will. "The parties of men cram their tenets down all men's throats whom they can get into their power, without permitting them to examine their truth or falsehood" (E IV.3.20, 552). And this tyranny over the mind is far worse than mere physical tyranny; "he is certainly the most subjected, who is so in his understanding" (E IV.20.6, 711). A tradition divorced from the sincere search for truth becomes merely arbitrary and tyrannical.

Others – who in Locke's time were given the derisive label "enthusiasts" – seek the truth in ecstatic or transcendent religious experiences, believing that they are receiving communications (or at least suggestions or indications) directly from God. The fundamental error that gives rise to this tendency is to understand faith and reason as opposites; Locke defines "enthusiasm" as "that which, laying by reason, would set up revelation without it" (E IV.19.2, 698).

Locke is not against religious feelings, since we ought to revere God. In his religious writings he confirms that God works spiritually in the hearts of believers, helping them to overcome sin and lead better lives (see R 246, 185–186). But it is one thing to believe, in general, that God does such things; it is another thing entirely to use that as an excuse to set up a feeling or intuition or religious experience of my own as though it were the voice of God. What Locke opposes – vehemently – is treating religious feelings and experiences as though they spoke for God or in any other way added to the information we have about God. Feeling a certain way about God, given what we know about him, is one thing; relying on our feelings as the *basis* of what we know about him is another.

So by its very nature, religious enthusiasm is divorced from the search for truth. It negates the role of the mind – the only faculty capable of carrying out the search. Using our minds to learn about God requires us to identify a source of communication from God that we have valid grounds to believe really comes from him. A religious feeling, simply by itself, could never meet that test – since feelings don't supply grounds or reasons for things.

But none of that causes any concern to the enthusiasts, because they have already laid aside reason. Enthusiasts thus believe that "whatever groundless opinion comes to settle itself strongly upon their fancies is an illumination from the spirit of God" (E IV.19.6, 699). Any idea, belief, feeling or conception that occurs strongly in their minds is validated as true simply because it occurs strongly in their minds. "They are sure because they are sure; and their persuasions are right, because they are strong in them" (E IV.19.9, 700).

Enthusiasm, in Locke's view, is far more dangerous than traditionalism. The enthusiast is even more liable to seek to impose his views on others by force (see E IV.19.2, 698). And the enthusiast will go to greater extremes. The traditionalist is at least limited by his tradition; the enthusiast is limited by nothing but the extent of his own imagination. "For strong conceit, like a new principle, carries all easily with it, when got above common sense and freed from all restraint of reason, and check of reflection" (E IV.19.7, 699).

Making matters worse, for the same reason enthusiasts are more likely to impose their beliefs on others and more likely to have extreme beliefs, they are also harder to persuade to change their minds. "The love of something extraordinary, the ease and glory it is to be inspired and be above the common and natural ways of knowledge, so flatters many men's laziness, ignorance and vanity, that when once they are got into this way of immediate revelation, of illumination without search, and of certainty without proof and without examination, 'tis a hard matter to get them out of it" (E IV.19.8, 700).

A third place people look for truth is by examining a sacred text. Locke himself followed this path extensively in his other writings, and in the *Essay* he explores some of the epistemological questions that lie behind this aspect of the search for truth. He believed that logic and evidence provided sufficient grounds to be certain that the Bible was God's word.

Searching for truth in the Bible plays an important role in Locke's effort to heal social fragmentation over religion. As we will see in Chapter 3, in his religious and political works he argued that the

Bible calls on all people to refrain from violent conflict over religion, and cultivate reason rather than fanaticism. The epistemology of the *Essay* provides much of the basis for Locke's approach to scripture in these writings.

But while analysis of the Bible is one way Locke argues for social healing, and these arguments even appear in his political works as well as in his religious works, he does not give the Bible a political role. That is, Locke does not want people's interpretations of the Bible imposed on others through the political system any more than he wants their traditions or religious enthusiasms imposed on others.

A proper approach to the Bible does not negate, but rather strongly affirms, the role of the mind and its reasoning faculties as the tool we use to interpret the language of the text. The Bible is therefore not inimical to the search for truth, as religious feelings (when detached from the Bible) are.

Yet the difficulties of interpreting language are often very great, and people can reasonably and sincerely disagree about the meaning of a text. "Though everything said in the text be infallibly true, yet the reader may be – nay, cannot chose but be – very fallible in the understanding of it. Nor is it to be wondered that the will of God, when clothed in words, should be liable to that doubt and uncertainty which unavoidably attends that sort of conveyance" (E III.9.23, 489–490). The difficulty of language is an extended theme in the *Essay*, taking up a large portion of the book.

Because of these difficulties, forcing one person to submit to another person's interpretation of a text would, in practice, divorce it from the sincere search for truth. "It would become us to be more charitable, one to another, in our interpretations or misunderstandings of those ancient writings" (E III.9.22, 489). For the person who is having others' views imposed on him, his own sincere search for truth and the interpretation others are forcing onto him would be in conflict.

The common theme that emerges in these various topics is the pervasive temptation to take things (like tradition, religious experience, or Bible study) that began as ways of searching for truth, but sacrifice the search itself to some other goal. Human beings find the search for truth uncomfortable and have a strong natural tendency to avoid it. They "worship the idols that have been set up in their minds" and "stamp the characters of divinity upon absurdities and errors" (E I.3.26, 83). And "those who affected to be masters and teachers" have always sought "to make this the principle of principles, that principles must not be questioned" (E I.4.24, 101).

Sometimes the motive to put other things ahead of the search for truth feels noble to the person who experiences it – such as the person who seeks to impose his beliefs on others out of a genuine desire that they might know the truth and be rescued from error. Sometimes the motive is something as simple as sloth and inattention – it's just easier not to examine our beliefs. A hunger for money and power are very often involved, since those who impose their beliefs on others gain a position of power by doing so. And many times the deepest motive is the most wicked of all – nothing is more flattering to human pride than the idea that God has chosen me, or my group, to have special possession of the truth that others have not been privileged to receive. The person who imposes beliefs on others is literally playing God.

iv. HOW THE TRUTH CAN UNITE US

But there is one way in which the search for truth can unite rather than divide, and do so in a specifically political way. That is through "natural reason," meaning the use of reason without the assistance of revelation from God (such as through scripture).

All people have reason and are capable of using it to investigate the fundamental questions. "Our business here [on earth] is not to know all things, but those which concern our conduct" (E I.1.6, 46). And for that purpose, natural reason will suffice. He writes of human beings in general that "how short soever their knowledge may come of a universal or perfect comprehension of whatsoever is, it yet secures their great concernments, that they have light enough to lead them to the knowledge of their maker, and the sight of their own duties" (E I.1.5, 45).

All the major social groups in Locke's time – Puritan, traditional Anglican, and Catholic – agreed that natural reason was a valid way of discerning truth from error, because it was planted in us by God. And, unlike biblical analysis, natural reason is not subject to the special difficulties that arise from interpreting texts. Natural reason could therefore produce consensus across fragmented groups. A belief or a rule of behavior justified by reason can become a shared basis for community life, because it can draw agreement from members of all groups.

And, as Locke would go on to argue in his political writings, natural reason uniquely justifies the use of force. If someone refuses to submit to your tradition, your religious enthusiasm, or your understanding of the Bible, that might be because he, after a sincere and good-faith consideration of the issues, disagrees with you. But if someone refuses to submit to clear and unambiguous reason, you are justified in proceeding on the assumption that he is being – well, unreasonable. Reason is "the common rule and measure God hath given mankind," therefore those who harm their neighbors in direct defiance of reason have "declared war against all mankind" and "may be destroyed as a lion or a tiger, one of those wild savage beasts with whom men can have no society or security" (T II.11, 120). ·

It is essential to note that the idea here is not to set up an opposition between reason and religion. As we will see at some length, the goal is precisely the opposite. Locke believes that reason and faith are perfectly compatible, and it is only because he believes this that he thinks he can offer rational arguments to religious people and expect to draw them together. The idea is to offer people claims based on reason that they will accept within the framework of their religions, not in opposition to them.

This was a promising method because all the main branches of Christianity held – and had held more or less consistently for over a thousand years – that reason and faith were not opposed to one another.[47] Roughly speaking, the majority opinion in Christianity has been that reason is the faculty by which the mind perceives truth, not only on its own ("natural reason") but also when exposed to a revelation from God that it has grounds to believe is genuine. Faith is the practice of actively following in your life what your reason tells you to be true (especially about God) even when you are tempted to abandon your beliefs.[48] (We will look at the relationship between reason and faith in much more detail in Chapter 3.)

It is not the job of the *Essay* to actually construct the rational arguments for beliefs and rules that can build social consensus. That is what Locke sets out to do in his religious and political works. The *Essay* provides the road map for how and why this task is to be done – to provide the intellectual basis for doing it.

This is why, as we noted at the beginning of this book, one Locke scholar commented that in reading the last portion of the *Essay*, "I felt myself present at the making of the modern mind."[49] One of the major reasons Locke has been so influential on what people in the modern world believe about God, about science, about politics, and so many other subjects is because of his influence, through the *Essay*, on how we think about belief itself.

v. THE LIMITS OF UNITY – AND THE LIMITS OF THE LIMITS

One of the most important aspects of the *Essay* is to discover the limits of what reason can do, to keep it modest. The effort to counter religious fanaticism with reason only works if reason itself does not become just another form of religious fanaticism. We must be careful not to take reason beyond its own natural limitations.

In the *Essay*, Locke attacks both medieval scholastics and Enlightenment rationalists who are so eager to solve problems with reason that they accept all kinds of weak arguments in its name. "Men, extending their inquiries beyond their capacities, and letting their thoughts wander into those depths where they can find no sure footing," is the reason "they raise questions and multiply disputes which, never coming to any clear resolution, are proper only to continue and increase their doubts and to confirm them at last in perfect skepticism" (E I.1.7, 47). Mapping out the limits of what we can and cannot establish by reason is one of the *Essay*'s major themes.

The major changes Locke introduces into epistemology all relate to these limits. He draws stricter boundaries than previous epistemologists had drawn on what we can know with great certainty by natural reason. He also draws stricter boundaries on our ability to interpret language with great certainty – with implications for religion insofar as Bible interpretation is impacted.

Locke emphasizes the moral duty of recognizing these limits. We do much harm to ourselves and even endanger our neighbors when we fail to regulate our beliefs in accordance with the real limits of our mental abilities. "The busy mind of man" should "be more cautious in meddling with things exceeding its comprehension; to stop when it is at the utmost extent of its tether, and sit down in a quiet ignorance of those things which, upon examination, are found to be beyond the reach of our capacities" (E I.1.4, 45).

But, most importantly, he lays out an argument for how, in spite of these limits, there are some beliefs – both in natural reason and in interpreting revelation – that we can hold with a very high degree of certainty. We can acknowledge the limits of natural reason and still believe in things based on it. We can acknowledge the limits of our ability to interpret scripture and still believe in things based on it.

You might say Locke believes so much in epistemological limits that he even believes there are limits to the limits. It's important to be epistemologically modest – but not *too* epistemologically modest.

The key to this outcome is Locke's emphasis on what he calls "degrees of assent." The fundamental commitment we must make in the search for truth is not simply to believe only the truth. It is to hold each particular belief with the level of certainty that is appropriate to the strength of our reasons for believing it (see E IV.16, 657–668). We must diligently distinguish not only between truth and error, but between which things we can be very sure are true and which things we are only somewhat sure are true.

If we do this, we will not only weaken our adherence to beliefs that are less certain, we will also strengthen our adherence to beliefs that are more certain. Far from indiscriminately reducing our confidence in all beliefs, Locke's emphasis on the limits of reason provide a sound basis for confidence that there are some things you really can know for sure (see E IV.17.16, 685).

It is worth noting that Locke's combination of an emphasis on limits and a firm assertion that there are nonetheless some things we can really know for sure is one reason why – as we will see in Chapter 6 – his epistemology lent itself to radical politics. Epistemological overconfidence lends itself to traditionalism and hence to political conservatism (as it did in Descartes) because if figuring things out is easy, it stands to reason that thousands of people passing down knowledge over centuries will produce more truth than any one person. And epistemological skepticism leads even more directly to political conservatism (as in David Hume) because if we don't know anything we have no basis on which to critique the existing order. However, if you think that knowing the truth is difficult, but not too difficult for us to succeed, you have a starting point for revolutionary politics.

vi.   YOU AREN'T BORN A BELIEVER, YOU'RE BORN TO BELIEVE

The *Essay* consists of four books, and the first book stands out from the others. Books II–IV are fairly systematic, laying out in logical order Locke's argument for how we should think about the way we process our ideas. Book I, by contrast, is entirely negative. It takes up an opposing view and argues at length against it.

It argues against the view that the human mind is born containing "innate principles." This is a subtle argument and the issues are widely misunderstood. The doctrine that there are "innate principles" in the human mind was widespread in Locke's day, but it has been out of favor for a long time, so the arguments Locke is responding to are no longer carefully studied by more than a handful of specialists. Thus most readers of the *Essay* today are in danger of misunderstanding the point if they don't read carefully.

Although today people usually describe the topic of Book I as being about innate "ideas," Locke's concern in this book is really about beliefs rather than ideas as such. He describes what he is arguing against as the doctrine of "innate principles." And he takes up this subject at such length because he thinks this is critical to understanding the right and wrong approach to examining our beliefs.

He is primarily responding to people who use the doctrine of "innate principles" to set up some beliefs as being naturally present in the human mind. Some examples of beliefs that people in Locke's time attributed to innate principles include the belief that two contradictory statements cannot both be true, or that we ought to do unto others as we would have them do unto us.

His main point is that people are not born already believing things. No one is born a believer – in anything. Propositions like " 'tis impossible for the same thing to be and not to be" may seem innate because no rational person could deny them. But if it were really innate, everyone would be aware of them, and "these propositions are so far from having a universal assent, that there are a great part of mankind to whom they are not so much as known" (E I.2.4, 49). Small children are the most obvious example (see E I.2.5, 49) but there are millions of people who pass their entire adulthood without ever becoming aware of principles like this, because they never think about them (see E I.2.12, 53). No one becomes aware of these principles until his mind is directed to examining them, and most people's minds never are. And if knowledge is "innate" simply because we discover it when we think about it, then every single piece of knowledge without exception is "innate" because that's how we discover all knowledge (see E.I.2.6–9, 51–52).

So Locke is not saying that there is no such thing as human nature or that the mind has no innate qualities or tendencies. Quite the contrary, Locke has very strong views on the natural tendencies of the human mind. For example, of the guiding ideas of his political philosophy is that people have a natural tendency toward selfishness, short-sightedness, and other socially dysfunctional behaviors.[50]

Instead, Locke is simply arguing that beliefs undergo a process of discovery and formation. The doctrine of "innate principles" implies that some beliefs transcend such processes. Locke wants to establish that all beliefs are subject to some sort of constructive process within the mind, by which the mind figures out what it believes.

As we have seen, the underlying problem for Locke in the *Essay* is that people have a natural tendency to avoid examining their beliefs. To avoid being forced to call their beliefs into question, they erect barriers that protect their thoughts from being challenged. Tearing those barriers down is one of the main purposes of the *Essay*.

Locke sees the doctrine of innate principles as one of the more insidious of these barriers. Many of the philosophical and theological systems of his time claimed to start with a set of beliefs supposedly derived from innate principles, and then reason from that starting point to a much larger set of principles. In the mind of the believer, the whole convoluted philosophical or theological system would take on the certainty associated with an innate principle.

This is not the same as saying the mind has no natural tendency to *form* beliefs, or even a natural tendency to form one particular belief rather than another. In fact, Locke argues that while we don't have innate "principles," we do have innate powers of reasoning and perception which will, in the usual course of things, lead us to believe specific things. It's not like the mind is somehow neutral between $2 + 2 = 4$ and $2 + 2 = 5$, making us equally receptive to believing either one. When Locke says, for example, that the principle that two contradictory statements cannot both be true is not an innate principle, he's not saying the mind has no innate tendency toward reaching that conclusion. He just means that we're not born already believing it – we have to go through a process of realization.

In short, we are not born believing, but we are born to believe. The mind has a natural power of distinguishing truth from error that naturally leads it to belief. "Though the comprehension of our understandings comes exceedingly short of the vast extent of things, yet we shall have cause enough to magnify the bountiful author of our being for that portion and degree of knowledge he has bestowed on us, so far above all the other inhabitants of this, our mansion" (E I.1.5, 45).

Thus, on one level, Locke's critique of innate principles doesn't go far beyond mere common sense. If by "innate principles" you mean that people are born already believing certain things, Locke thinks that's just obviously not true. On the other hand, if by "innate principles" you only mean that people have an innate *tendency* toward realizing certain conclusions – well, that's true, but it's not a very profound observation, so why are you making such a big deal of it?

However, there is a more weighty point at stake. Insisting that all beliefs come from a process of realization is critical for Locke because it implies that all beliefs are open to examination. If all beliefs are produced by a process rather than being innate, then for any given belief we can go back and walk ourselves through the process retroactively – suspend the belief and see if we can, so to speak, re-create it, starting only with other beliefs that we are already certain of, and without embracing any logical errors, unwarranted inferences, etc.

vii. THE LIMITS OF IDEAS

With Book II, the positive argument of the *Essay* begins. Having established that "ideas" are not innate – at least not in the sense of being already consciously present from birth – Locke naturally turns to the question of how they're formed.

Locke defines an "idea" as anything the mind is directly aware of or thinking about. He argues that they arise from two sources, which he calls "sensation" and "reflection." Sensation just means the input of the five senses, and reflection is the mind's perception of its own operations, such as thinking, believing, willing, feeling, etc. – a sort of inner version of sensation. He provides a detailed account (which we need not review here) of the various different types of ideas in each of these categories, and of how simpler ideas combine to form more complex mental structures.

Locke's emphasis on the central importance of ideas in epistemology was unprecedented. No one had ever consistently spoken of "ideas" in the sense Locke gave this term.[51] The important difference between Locke and his predecessors was that he systematically separated the activity of thinking not only from objects outside the mind being thought about, but also from the object of thought inside the mind.[52] So, for example, as I sit here at my computer typing these words, most epistemologists would say that I am aware of the computer. Locke would say I am aware of the idea of the computer – my eyes generate an image of the computer in my mind, and that's what I'm aware of. There is an intermediate step between my mind and the computer, and that is what "ideas" are.

Locke's critics, from his own time down to the present day, complain that if ideas are an intermediary between us and the world around us, we have no way to be sure that there really is a world around us at all.[53] On Locke's view, we can never mentally connect to the world, we can only connect to the ideas that occur in our minds, which we trust come to us from an outside world.

But Locke, as we have already observed, simply isn't worried about this problem. "The certainty of things existing *in rerum natura* [i.e. "in the nature of things," really existing rather than only appearing to exist] when we have the testimony of our senses for it, is not only as great as our frame can attain to, but as our condition needs" (E IV.11.8, 634).

For those who are not inclined to question whether there really is an objective world, the distinction between thought and ideas is useful for examining the limits of our mental capacities. This is exactly why Locke draws it. He wants to ask what objects we are and are not capable of fully understanding given the ideas we are able to form.

To take one of the more important topics in the *Essay* as an example of how Locke's language of "ideas" helps examine our mental limits: Locke points out (as very many had done before) that our minds are not capable of fully understanding God, because God is infinite and our finite minds cannot contain an infinite idea (see E II.17.1, 210; II.17.17, 219–220; and II.17.20, 221–222). We are, of course, capable of understanding some things about God. For example, we can understand that he is infinite, because we do have an adequate idea of what "infinity" itself is – the absence of limitations. But we cannot actually contemplate an infinite object, which is a very different thing from understanding what "infinity" is. And because we cannot contemplate an infinite object, our understanding of God is limited.

More controversially, Locke argues that there is much we cannot understand about our own mental and spiritual natures – in brief, about thought and the soul – because we cannot form an adequate idea of them. To do so, our minds would have to, so to speak, step outside thought and the soul themselves in order to examine them. A mind attempting to fully understand itself is like an eardrum attempting to hear itself or a taste bud attempting to taste itself. Locke rebukes some of the prevailing schools of philosophical and theological thought, especially Descartes and his followers, for asserting things about the nature of thought and the soul that no one could possibly have grounds for knowing.

Take, for example, Descartes' infamous assertion that because the essence of the soul is thinking, the soul must always think, even when we're unconscious. How does Descartes know that the essence of the soul is thinking? " 'Tis doubted whether I thought all last night or no; the question being about a matter of fact, 'tis begging it, to bring as a proof of it a hypothesis which is the very thing in dispute." If we can follow a method like this, we could prove that pocket-watches think constantly as long as their gears continue to move, by defining the movement of the gears as thinking (E II.1.10, 109).

Again, as with the infinity of God, this does not mean there is nothing about thinking or the soul that we can understand. We have direct, experiential knowledge of our capacity for thinking and will-ing. And in particular, if we reflect on these capacities, we will see that we could not possibly think and will if there were nothing going on in us but mere motions of matter. The idea that matter could think without the intervention of some sort of metaphysical com-ponent is inconsistent with what we know (from reflection) about the act of thinking. "It is for want of reflection that we are apt to think that our senses show us nothing but material things. Every act of sensation, when duly considered, gives us an equal view of both parts of nature, the corporeal and spiritual." This is because "whilst I know by seeing and hearing, etc., that there is some corporal being without me ... I do more certainly know that there is some spiritual being within me that sees and hears" (E II.23.15, 305–306). Our material bodies could not see and hear, much less think rationally, without some spiritual component, because "cognition" is "not within the natural powers of matter" (E IV.3.6, 542).[54]

But in Locke's view, while we can know that we have souls because we couldn't think without them, trying to build a metaphysical account of the nature of the soul is something our minds aren't equipped to do. He refers to "this ignorance we are in of the nature of that thinking thing that is in us, and which we look on as ourselves" (E II.27.27, 347). We are not ignorant of its existence, but we are ignorant of its nature. Schools of thought that claim to understand the metaphysics of the soul – whether philosophical or theological in orientation – are a prime example of people stubbornly pushing beyond what they have a right to claim to know. And that sets the stage for social conflict, since these claims about the soul are religiously divisive.

Far more important for Locke than the metaphysics of the soul is its immortality. As we have noted, he is relentlessly concerned to prioritize questions that "concern our conduct" and leave aside merely speculative matters. And when it comes to guiding our conduct, fine-spun speculations about whether the soul still thinks while we're unconscious pale to insignificance next to the great question of whether the soul still thinks after we're dead. Those who spend their time trying to disentangle the metaphysics of the soul's nature are distracting attention from the more urgent question of its destiny.

Traditionally, in western philosophy, going back to Plato's *Phaedo*, the subject of the soul's metaphysics has been raised precisely as a way of proving that the soul lives on after death. But Locke sees no reason we would need a metaphysics of the soul to believe in the afterlife, and thinks that in fact, the whole subject of metaphysics is a distraction. This is not a question for speculative reason but for theology. If we can rationally justify belief that the Bible is God's word – and, as we will see later, Locke thinks we can – then that will be the proper ground for believing in the soul's mmortality. For Christians, "it is evident that he who made us at first begin to subsist here [as] sensible, intelligent beings ... can and will restore us to the like state of sensibility in another world," so " 'tis not of such mighty necessity to determine one way or the other" on questions about the soul's metaphysics (E IV.3.6, 542).

viii. THE LIMITS OF LANGUAGE

The last chapter of Book II is about what Locke calls "the association of ideas."[55] The mind produces beliefs by forming mental associations between ideas when it perceives, or assumes, that they are naturally connected (E II.33.5, 395). For example, when a child is first presented with the formula $2 + 2 = 4$, his mind manipulates the idea of "2" and the idea of "4" in order to compare "2 + 2" with "4," and upon making the comparison he perceives that these ideas do, in fact, naturally correspond in such a way that the idea "2 + 2" is identical to the idea "4." He then forms a mental association between those two ideas such that, in the future, he doesn't need to perform the whole comparison over again; he simply associates "2 + 2" with "4" in that relation by habit.

At the end of Book II, Locke notes that, now that he's laid out what ideas are, we might naturally expect him to move on to look at how the mind processes them to produce beliefs. But first he has another topic to take up, because there is another, equally important source of epistemological limitations besides the limits of ideas. That is the limitations of language, which are the subject of Book III.

The great danger is that faulty or careless use of language can cause us to form associations among ideas without realizing we are doing so. Thus we think we are thinking about one object when in fact we are thinking about another.

The use of language requires the person speaking to make two assumptions about the words he is using. Both of these assumptions are opportunities for error. If we make the assumption erroneously, we introduce false associations of ideas without realizing it.

The first assumption is that the idea corresponding to a given word in the speaker's mind is the same as the idea corresponding to that word in the audience's mind. For example, if you and I talk about our friend John, I assume that what I mean by "our friend John" and what you mean by "our friend John" is the same thing. But if I'm thinking about John Smith and you're thinking about John Jones, we will talk at cross-purposes. If neither of us happens to mention the last name, we may cause big trouble. If I tell you "John" stole something, you will erroneously associate the theft with John Jones, who is innocent.

The other assumption the speaker must make is that the idea corresponding to a given word in his mind also corresponds to a real object. In other words, the speaker must assume that his idea of the thing the word refers to is accurate. If the only dogs I have ever seen are large brown dogs, and I assume all dogs are like that, I will erroneously associate the ideas of large size and brown color with the word "dog," when they ought not to be associated with it because those ideas are not true of all dogs. I may say things about "dogs" that aren't true, and misunderstand what I hear others saying about "dogs."

Failure to understand the limitations of language is just as dangerous as failure to understand the limitations of ideas. Locke discusses a number of different contexts in which confused language has led to social conflict.

Locke again notes that people naturally dislike having their ideas challenged and tend to find ways to insulate their beliefs from examination. Abuse of the limitations of language is one of the major strategies people employ to block the process of fair scrutiny.

The most prominent example Locke takes up is that of the medieval scholastic movement. In particular, the scholastics sought to learn about the natural world by dividing things up into categories, called "species," and then listing the qualities that defined the "essence" of each species. So, for example, four-leggedness is part of the essence of the species "dog," because all dogs are naturally four-legged (though of course they can lose their limbs). But brownness is not part of the essence of dogness because not all dogs are brown.

Locke wrote that this whole approach to nature was wrongheaded and had impeded the progress of true science – the scholastics, whose thought continued to dominate the curriculum in the universities, had "very much perplexed the knowledge of natural things" (E III.3.17, 418). Armchair philosophers sitting up in their ivory towers deciding what qualities were or were not "essential" to each "species" were just moving words around, not learning about the world as it really was. Worse, they were creating rigid categories of thought that would limit our ability to learn from experience. Locke did not deny that each object had some kind of "essence" or "substance" of which it was made, but he thought we should not reify these concepts into rigid categories, because we lack the power to directly perceive these essences. He subscribed to the emerging Enlightenment theory that the real "essence" of physical objects would truly be found in a microscopic structure of millions upon millions of unimaginably tiny particles from which material objects were made.[56]

In addition to its implications for science, medieval essentialism had implications for religion and politics. The assertions of the scholastics about the essences of objects naturally led to assertions about the appropriate way to treat those objects – their proper place in the universe and in our lives. The scholastics believed that God had made a universe relatively transparent to the human intellect, such that it wasn't very difficult – at least for intellectuals like themselves – to know the real nature of things and therefore their appropriate uses.[57]

Locke saw this whole approach as merely a clever way for the professional intellectual class to accumulate power and influence. Locke writes of the "artificial ignorance, and learned gibberish" that prevail "in these last ages, by the interest and artifice of those who found no easier way to that pitch of authority and dominion they have attained" (E III.10.9, 495). The real workings of the physical universe are much too mysterious, in Locke's view, for anyone to put himself in the position of claiming to have deciphered it.

Another implication of Locke's treatment of language in the *Essay* is, as we have already suggested, the limitation it places on the role of the Bible in politics. Because it is easy to misunderstand – or twist – the meaning of words, we should not be surprised if people interpret biblical passages in a variety of ways even when the passages are in fact fairly straightforward and the meaning is clear to a careful and attentive reader. "What have the greatest part of the comments and disputes upon the laws of God and man served for, but to make the meaning more doubtful, and perplex the sense?" (E III.10.12, 496).

ix. REASONS TO BELIEVE – JUDGMENT AND DEGREES OF ASSENT

Having covered all this ground to make us aware of the limits of our ideas, in Book IV Locke turns to the subject of how we can know and believe things in spite of those limits.

Following a centuries-old custom – one that started falling out of use not long after his time – Locke speaks of "knowledge" and "belief" as two sharply distinct things. Knowledge is the direct perception of relationships between our ideas, such as the mind directly perceiving that $2 + 2 = 4$ or that if $A = B$ and $B = C$, then $A = C$. Knowledge is therefore never subject to uncertainty; it is always absolutely certain.

Belief, on the other hand, involves making at least some assumptions about the relationships between ideas rather than directly perceiving them. For example, I cannot directly perceive that flipping the light switch causes the light to turn on. I believe that flipping the switch turns on the light because I assume that there is a causal connection between the idea of flipping the switch and the idea of the light coming on. All thinking about the world outside our minds requires this assumption-making process to some extent.

Belief, obviously, can be subject to uncertainty if we make assumptions that aren't certain. But although Locke speaks in terms of this medieval distinction between knowledge and belief, he strongly emphasizes that we should not think beliefs are always less certain than knowledge.

Some beliefs are so sure that they are, in effect, just as certain as knowledge. "Sometimes ... the probability is so clear and strong that assent as necessarily follows it, as knowledge follows demonstration" (E IV.17.16, 685). Technically I do not "know" that there is such a place as China or that physical objects do not vanish when I'm not looking at them and then reappear when I look at them again; I only "believe" these things. But beliefs like these are so certain that they effectively function as though they were knowledge (see E IV.16.8, 662).

Locke thinks epistemologists are wasting their time when they worry about whether we can ever be really, fully certain of some beliefs. "He that in the ordinary affairs of life would admit of nothing but direct, plain demonstration, would be sure of nothing in this world but of perishing quickly" (E IV.11.10, 636).

This emphasis demonstrates, again, the distinctive nature of Locke's interest in epistemology. Locke's critics attack him for not being able to justify this assertion that belief can be as certain as knowledge, because – by Locke's own admission – we have no basis for directly examining assumptions such as the one in the light-switch example above.[58] But just as Locke is not interested in painstaking investigations of his own existence or the existence of the objective world, he is also not interested in painstaking investigations of whether light switches really do turn on lights. That kind of question is simply beside his purpose. Given that we do, in fact, make assumptions such as this, how can we responsibly regulate the way we act on them? That is Locke's question.

Locke defines reason as the faculty that draws connections between ideas, producing both knowledge and belief. When reason perceives the connections directly, it produces knowledge. When we must make assumptions about the connections, reason exercises what Locke calls "judgment." This produces belief (see E IV.14–15).

To exercise good judgment is to make assumptions about connections between ideas in a responsible way. We must consider how probable our assumptions are to be true, and proceed with due certainty, or due caution, depending on that consideration. "The grounds of probability ... as they are the foundations on which our assent is built, so are they the measure whereby its several degrees are, or ought to be, regulated" (E IV.16.1, 657).

This idea of "degrees of assent" is critical to Locke's approach to responsible belief formation. Good judgment does not just involve deciding whether or not to make a given assumption about the connection between ideas. It also involves deciding how certain we can be about the assumption if we do make it, and then remaining mindful of that certainty level afterwards. If the assumption is highly certain (such as that light switches turn on lights) good judgment calls on us to treat the resulting beliefs as highly certain – treat them with a high "degree of assent" or level of agreement. But we cannot go through life only making the very highly certain assumptions; to live in this world we have to make many assumptions that are less certain. Good judgment requires us to treat the resulting beliefs with a lower degree of assent – to be mindful of the uncertainty that lies behind our own thinking on those subjects.

Because reason is the faculty that regulates our beliefs in this way, Locke argues that "reason must be our last judge and guide in everything" (E IV.19.14, 704). Reason is our only hope for responsible behavior, because only reason distinguishes between more and less certain beliefs, so we can know when to proceed with caution (because we cannot be as sure of what we believe) and when to charge ahead (because we can).

And because each person can only be certain of his own beliefs insofar as he has used his own reason, yet each person is limited in his ability to rationally analyze his own beliefs, there is always necessarily a lot of uncertainty in the world. This becomes a key argument for toleration and general goodwill toward people of differing beliefs:

It is unavoidable to the greatest part of men, if not all, to have several opinions without certain and indubitable proofs of their truths; and it carries too great an imputation of ignorance, lightness or folly for men to quit and renounce their former tenets presently upon the offer of an argument which they cannot immediately answer and show the insufficiency of: it would, methinks, become all men to maintain peace, and the common offices of humanity and friendship, in the diversity of opinions, since we cannot reasonably expect that anyone should readily and obsequiously quit his own opinion and embrace ours with a blind resignation to an authority which the understanding of man acknowledges not. (E IV.16.4, 659–660)

The culmination of the *Essay* is a treatment of how we can rationally investigate the most important of all questions: what to believe about God. We will look at this topic in detail in Chapter 3, in the context of a broader consideration of Locke's religion. But it is worth noting here that after Locke has laid out how and why he thinks reason should regulate belief, religion is the only subject to which he then applies this method. This, above all things, is what "concerns our conduct."

x. EPISTEMOLOGY AND POLITICS

As we will see in later chapters, Locke's political theory follows a consensus-building method. He seeks to build politics on moral rules that are shared across religious groups. To do this, he must maintain a strategic silence about beliefs that are not shared across groups. He relies on the fact that Puritans, traditional Anglicans and Catholics all believe in roughly the same rules of social conduct; he doesn't mention the theological and metaphysical issues on which they disagree. As one scholar puts it, Locke's political writings make moral appeals calculated to produce "minimum controversy and maximum appeal."[59]

This doesn't mean Locke's theory is philosophically superficial. Locke's moral appeals have deep philosophical roots; he just confines them to topics of widespread agreement. Rather than try to persuade you to abandon your whole worldview and adopt a new one, he seeks to show you that your worldview (whatever it is) includes moral premises that, when followed out faithfully, should lead you to his conclusions.

This method grows out of his epistemology. Locke is using his fundamental commitment to degrees of assent and other epistemological premises to resettle the boundary between what in the political community is shared, and what is private. Your metaphysical speculations may concern an important topic – God – but how sure can you be of beliefs arrived at in this way? Is it reasonable for you to impose your interpretation of a biblical text on others when they interpret it differently than you do?

And Locke is relying on the premise that what is really known for certain by natural reason will also be widely shared across religious groups. What is not known for certain will not be shared, because different people's judgments will differ. Even things that are known for certain from revelation will not be shared across groups, because the difficulties of language are such that careless reading will lead many people astray even in interpreting the most clear-cut Bible passages. But, for example, we know for sure by natural reason that murder and theft are wrong, and – surprise, surprise – it just so happens that all cultural groups happen to share that premise. Natural reason is not only philosophically sound, it's socially sound.

CHAPTER 3

LOCKE'S REASONABLE FAITH

In Book IV of the *Essay Concerning Human Understanding*, after laying out the definition of reason we have reviewed in Chapter 2, Locke makes this comment: "There is another use of the word reason, wherein it is opposed to faith." This is "in itself a very improper way of speaking," but the habit of speaking of reason and faith as opposites is so common that "it would be folly either to oppose or hope to remedy it" (E IV.17.24, 687).

Yet that "folly" is exactly what Locke goes on to attempt, at some length, in the remainder of the *Essay*. He argues that faith and reason are not just compatible, but natural complements – even interdependent, to some extent.

Locke's observation that it is common to talk about faith and reason as opposites – so much so that only a fool would try to persuade people to speak otherwise – was exaggerated. In fact, for over a thousand years, the predominant view had been precisely the opposite; as far back as the early fifth century, Augustine of Hippo, perhaps the most important theologian in Christian history, wrote that he would make his case on a particular subject "not merely by appealing to divine authority, but also by employing such powers of reason as we can apply for the benefit of unbelievers."[60] This view had been codified in the great magisterial works of the medieval scholastics and reaffirmed by the leaders of the Reformation as well. And many other people besides Locke in seventeenth-century England still spoke of faith and reason as partners.

Nonetheless, Locke had reason to be daunted about the prospects for getting people to think of reason and faith in this way. During the seventeenth century the influence of the Enlightenment, especially from the Continent in places like France, was issuing a major challenge to the view of faith and reason as natural allies. It had become common to talk about reason as the opposite of faith on both sides of the divide – as the anti-religious philosophers of the Continental Enlightenment promoted reason against faith, many religious thinkers responded by promoting faith against reason.

This challenge to the old way of thinking about reason and faith as partners threatened to cast doubt on the reasonableness of Christianity. Could a rational person believe in Christ? The relationship between reason and faith has always been fertile ground for philosophers and theologians, but never more than at this historical moment.

What was required – and what many Christian writers of the time, including Locke, sought to provide – was a systematic reassessment of the rational grounds for belief. Of course there was nothing new about systematic apologetics; theologians in earlier centuries had certainly faced their challenges. The apologetic treatises of the early church against the persecuting Roman emperors, those of the Middle Ages advocating Christianity against Islam, and those of the sixteenth century defending historic Christian theology against radical movements that sprang up in the wake of the Reformation, all show that the theologians had never had things easy. But they hadn't been under the same pressure to challenge all their assumptions and justify all their claims.

In past ages, the main opponents to whom Christian theologians had been responding were always themselves religious people. The early church responded to the worshippers of Jupiter and Apollo and the other traditional Roman gods; the medieval theologians responded to Islam; the sixteenth-century theologians to unorthodox movements like Socinianism. There had always been atheists, deists, and others questioning revealed religion, but they had never been the main challengers, and they had never had the level of social and intellectual respectability they now had. The seventeenth-century challenge was new, and required a new kind of response.

Locke wanted to respond by showing that Christianity fully withstood the test of reason. The rational person could not only believe it, but believe it with great certainty. Indeed, on Locke's view, because the logic and evidence point unambiguously to Christianity, the more rational a person is, the more sure he should be that Christianity is true.

And although he was not the only Christian writer of this period to argue for a reconciliation of reason and faith, he was the one whose approach has been the most widely influential. Locke's account of why we should treat reason and faith as partners was the single most important and influential legacy of the *Essay* – and given the *Essay*'s landmark influence on subjects as diverse as natural science and the metaphysics of the soul, that is saying a great deal.

But that was only one side of his desire to show the compatibility of reason and faith. The other side was to advocate a more rational attitude among Christians about how to deal with differences in belief. As Locke took the approach to reason and faith he outlined in the *Essay* and put it into practice in his more directly religious writings, he built another landmark legacy: a systematic theological case for tolerance and Christian ecumenism that continues to broadly shape Christian attitudes to this day.

i.   LOCKE'S LOCKEAN RELIGION

Describing Locke's religious works is difficult for several reasons. One is that his beliefs don't fit into any of the standard theological categories. He borrowed ideas and influences from a wide variety of Christian traditions, and the combined result doesn't closely resemble any of them. In the preface to his most important theological work, he writes that he wrote the book because "the little satisfaction and consistency that is to be found in most of the systems of divinity [i.e. schools of theology] I have met with made me betake myself to the sole reading of the scriptures (to which they all appeal) for the understanding of the Christian religion" (R Preface, xxvii).

So scholars have never managed to settle on a label to describe Locke's theology. Some call him a Calvinist, but with some important qualifications; others call him a Latitudinarian with evangelical tendencies; others associate him with Socinianism, with the small caveat that he happened to disagree with almost all of the Socinian theological platform.[61] But each of these attempts to describe him is likely to be more misleading than helpful. Probably the only safe thing to say is that Locke's theology is Lockean.

Another problem is that Locke, in his mature works, remained silent about his beliefs on several of the central questions of Christian theology. While at Oxford, Locke held conventional Anglican theological principles on these questions, but later in life he avoided writing about them. We can speculate as to what he thought, and there are several plausible theories about that. We can also speculate as to why he remained silent, and there are several plausible theories about that, too. But if we wish to avoid speculation, we can provide at best a partial picture of his theology.

But the most difficult problem in describing Locke's religious works is the intersection of his religious motivations and his political motivations. One of the central ideas in Locke's political philosophy is that religious belief is a perennial source of social conflict. Society requires enforcement of moral rules, and what people believe about God is what shapes the moral rules they obey. And the central problem Locke has set himself to solve is the conflict over religion in his own time.

So Locke's writings about religion serve a double purpose. On the one hand, they are religious writings. Locke was a pious man, especially in the later part of his life when his major works were being published. When he writes about God, he is not constructing a theory about what kind of belief in God would be socially useful, assuming we could choose what to believe in. He is writing about the God he worships; he believes God has spoken in the Bible; and he is laying out what he understands God to have said.[62]

On the other hand, Locke's writings on religion are also a part of his political project. Or perhaps it would be better to say that Locke's project to build peace among competing religious groups was simultaneously political and religious. In its political aspect, the project was to find a way for these groups to live in peace in spite of their divisions. In its religious aspect, it was to persuade them not to be so deeply divided.

Locke sought to make the case to believers in all the major branches of Christianity that their faith required them not only to support toleration, but to view members of the other branches as their brothers and sisters in Christ. To Locke, going to the Bible to make the case for religious toleration in the civil sphere and spiritual unity in the church sphere was just as important as making the philosophical case for civil peace. And he didn't separate the two forms of argument, but placed them side by side as mutually reinforcing.

ii. REASONABLENESS IN OUR FAITH

As we saw in Chapter 2, the great message in which the *Essay* culminates is that reason must regulate all our beliefs, because that is the only way to be sure we believe and behave responsibly. This regulation consists not simply in sorting beliefs into two categories, "true" and "false," but in subdividing the "true" category by degrees of certainty. We have a responsibility to bring our behavior into line with the certainty of each belief – to treat the highly certain beliefs in practice as highly certain, and the less certain beliefs as less certain.

All this applies as much to faith as to any other topic. "Faith is nothing but a firm assent of the mind; which, if it be regulated as is our duty, cannot be afforded to anything but upon good reason" (E IV.17.24, 687).

In other words, to speak of "reason" and "faith" as having nothing to do with one another is to treat faith as though it were not a belief, since our powers of reason are where all our beliefs come from. "He that takes away reason to make way for revelation puts out the light of both, and does much the same as if he would persuade a man to put out his eyes, the better to receive the remote light of an invisible star by a telescope" (E IV.19.4, 698). It is through reason that we believe anything at all, just as it is through our eyes that we see anything at all. A revelation from God, such as the Bible, only makes new information available for our reason to believe, just as a telescope makes new sights visible to our eyes. The real issue is not whether we will use reason in forming our beliefs, but whether we will use it well or poorly.

Once the existence of a creator God is established (a subject we will look at below), it follows pretty quickly that God gave us reason precisely for the purpose of regulating beliefs. That is the function he made it and gave it to us, and he expects us to use it for that purpose. God has given each person "discerning faculties ... to keep him out of mistake and error," so "he that believes without having any reason for believing may be in love with his own fancies, but neither seeks truth as he ought nor pays the obedience due his maker" (E IV.17.24, 687–688) Thus, ultimately, the more reasonable we are in our faith, the more we carry out our duty to God.

Yet the temptation to escape the scrutiny of reason is strong. Thus, people typically make use of reason insofar as it benefits them, but then, when their own sacred cows come under examination, they suddenly discover that reason isn't relevant to the question. "I find every sect, as far as reason will help them, make use of it gladly; and where it fails them, they cry out, *'tis a matter of faith, and above reason*" (E IV.18.2, 689).

So far this case is general in nature – the case for reasonableness in our faith is the same as the case for reasonableness in every other aspect of our life, belief, and behavior. But Locke also goes on to review some considerations that are particular to the topic of religion. Two of the more important ones are challenges to putting reason in the ultimate place Locke wants it to have. One is a challenge on behalf of tradition, and the other is a challenge on behalf of having nothing at all in a position to ultimately regulate faith.

Against those who would make tradition the ultimate standard of faith, Locke argues that this implicitly divorces faith from truth. There are many traditions in the world; how do I know which is the one that contains the truth – or, if they all have some truth, which contains the most truth? If I put myself in the position of evaluating their merits and choosing between them, then I am using my reason to judge them, and reason rather than tradition is the ultimate standard. If tradition were really the ultimate standard, then "men have reason to be heathens in Japan, Mahumetans [i.e. Muslims] in Turkey, Papists in Spain, Protestants in England, and Lutherans in Sweden" (E IV.15.6, 657).

But an even more important challenge comes from those – the "enthusiasts" – who treat faith as an autonomous faculty that can perceive truth on its own. This essentially sets up faith as a new version of reason, performing the same function as reason (producing beliefs) but independently from it, and with different results than we get if we rely on reason.

On this view, because faith stands in the place of reason, faith is what we ought to look to as the ruling power in the soul. For the enthusiast, faith performs the function Locke ascribes to reason: regulating our beliefs. And naturally if faith performs the regulating function, nothing can regulate faith – otherwise that, and not faith, would be the regulating function.

The root problem with enthusiasm is that we do not in fact have any ability to perceive truth other than through reason. By setting aside reason, the enthusiast leaves himself with no regulating faculty at all. What he thinks is a regulating faculty is simply his moment-to-moment emotions and intuitions – which we have no reason to think are any more likely to point toward truth than error. The enthusiast not only "does violence to his own faculties" and "tyrannizes over his own mind," he also "usurps the prerogative that belongs to truth alone, which is to command assent by only its own authority" (E IV.19.2, 698).

Because the enthusiast has abandoned the only possible regulating faculty, there is no arguing with him. There is no common ground on which to meet him for discussion; there is no standard by which to measure the validity of his belief, since the belief is its own standard. The enthusiast's inward feeling of certainty is, by itself, self-validating – if he feels sure, that gives him valid grounds to be sure. "They are sure because they are sure; and their persuasions are right, because they are strong in them" (E IV.19.9, 700).

Enthusiasm is especially dangerous because, when it knocks down all limitation and regulation on belief, it knocks down all limitation and regulation on how we treat others. If the enthusiast should ever feel that he ought to impose his beliefs on others, there are no possible grounds for persuading him not to do so. The enthusiast has a built-in tendency toward "assuming an authority of dictating to others. ... For how, almost, can it be otherwise, but that he should be ready to impose on others' belief, who has already imposed on his own?" (E IV.19.2, 698).

There is only one solution – to persuade people not to be enthusiasts in the first place. Hence the primary place Locke gives to epistemology; if people don't get that right, there's no arguing with them later.

iii.   FAITHFULNESS IN OUR REASON

The partnership between reason and faith is a two-way street. While arguing against those who would make faith and reason opposites in order to exalt faith to the exclusion of reason, Locke also argues against those who would do so in order to exalt reason to the exclusion of faith.

The most important way in which people have a tendency to exclude faith in the name of reason is by denying the possibility or the relevance of revelation. Some hold that any form of belief that God has revealed something to humanity – say, the belief that the Bible is God's word – is inimical to reason. By accepting anything as a revelation from God, we have created a belief that reason doesn't regulate.

But Locke sees no contradiction between reason and revelation. "Reason is natural revelation," and "revelation is natural reason enlarged by a new set of discoveries" (E IV.19.4, 698). That is, what we know by natural reason, we only know because God chose to reveal it to us through natural reason; and when we receive revelation from a source like the Bible, our reason is the faculty that perceives, interprets, and understands the revelation, so our natural reason is not negated, nor even supplanted or complemented, but rather "enlarged."

There are no rational grounds for saying that God could not or would not reveal something to us. And if he did, there would be nothing irrational about accepting it – as long as we only accepted messages as revelations when we had rational grounds for confirming that they really were revealed by God. And Locke thinks we can have such grounds, for reasons we will look at below.

Another, closely related problem is the tendency to adopt only the portions of a revelation that can be independently confirmed by reason. This assumes that God would never reveal anything to us that we couldn't figure out on our own – an assumption that is unwarranted.

Right after Locke declares that "reason must be our last judge and guide in everything," he quickly adds this clarification: "I do not mean that we must consult reason and examine whether a proposition revealed from God can be made out by natural principles, and if it cannot, that then we may reject it" (E IV.19.14, 704). The role of reason is to judge whether the "proposition" in question is, or is not, actually a revelation from God. Once reason has certified the authenticity of the revelation, we must accept its content as true whether or not we can discern its truth independently. If God spoke, it would only be natural for him to tell us things we couldn't have figured out on our own. That's what would make revelation valuable.

At bottom, Locke thinks that these positions upholding faith alongside reason are nothing more than reasonableness itself demands. It would make no sense to decide for ourselves in advance – before having investigated the evidence – whether God has spoken to humanity, or what he would say if he did speak. We must go find out whether God speaks. And if God speaks, we must hear what he actually does say.

Thus, if God has spoken to humanity (as Locke thinks he has) then reason needs faith even to be reason, just as much as faith needs reason even to be faith. In the metaphor noted above, where our eyes stand for reason and the telescope stands for faith, the point is that faith cannot even be faith without the belief-forming power of reason. But, on the other side, reason is not reasonable if it begins by shutting out whole areas of truth because we don't want to give the evidence a fair hearing, or because we think we're so smart that an infinite, all-knowing God would have nothing to tell us that we couldn't have figured out for ourselves.

Also, Locke's insistence that reason should be the ultimate regulator of belief rather than tradition or religious experience does not mean he opposes either of those aspects of life altogether. As we have noted in Chapter 2, Locke was not a fan of traditions. Yet he also acknowledged that there is a limit to the amount of rational investigation any person can engage in, and that most people (who need to work for a living doing something other than conducting rational investigation of truth) will not have the time and capacity to do much rational investigating at all, beyond their basic duties to know God and the moral law (see E IV.20.2, 707).

For these cases, we have little choice but to fall back on received opinion – in effect, on tradition. "Indeed there are millions of truths that a man is not, or may not think himself, concerned to know," Locke writes. "There, 'tis not strange that the mind should give itself up to the common opinion" (E IV.20.16, 717).

Similarly, Locke does not reject all religious experience as inauthentic (see R 246, 185–186). His only concern is that reason must regulate the way we act on it. For example, suppose I have a gambling problem, and one day I have a religious experience and I believe God is helping me overcome my problem. If I stop gambling too much as a result of this experience, there's nothing in such an outcome that is contrary to reason – quite the contrary! But if I go on to believe that God is calling on me to burn down casinos, reason tells me that this belief must be mistaken. God would never call me to burn down casinos, since he has already shown me (both through natural reason and through the Bible) that such behavior is wrong.

Finally, the partnership between faith and reason rules out the possibility of "compartmentalizing" faith to one area of our lives. Those who see faith as the enemy of reason often want to exclude any influence of faith in areas of life that are felt to be reason's rightful territory, such as politics. This is one argument for religious freedom that has emerged in the last two centuries.

However, those are not the grounds on which Locke argued for religious freedom. This approach would be inconsistent with his argument for making faith reasonable. His case for this position is that there is nothing special about faith – it must submit to rational regulation like everything else. But if there is nothing special about faith, there are no special grounds for excluding it from any area of life. The flip side of making faith consistently reasonable is that reason must be consistently faithful to whatever it discovers about God.

Locke even offers an argument in one of his later books that the compartmentalization approach – drawing a separate sphere of reason and sphere of faith in human activities – always produces the triumph of irrational faith over faithless reason the life of society. Historically, Locke argues, societies that have divided faith from reason have been dominated by a power struggle between the priest-hood class and the political class. Both have a strong tendency to corruption and to cynical manipulation of the public, because each lacks the internal influence of the faculty (faith or reason) that belongs to the other; neither faith nor reason can be kept pure and honest without one another's influence. And in the end, the priests always turn out to be stronger than the politicians, because the over-whelming majority of the people are – and rightly so – more worried about getting right with God (or the gods) than they are about political and social concerns (R 238–241, 165–172).

Locke has other grounds for arguing that government should not enforce matters of faith. His approach is not to separate what is based on reason from what is based on faith, but rather to separate what is naturally shared among all human beings from what is not naturally shared among all human beings. As we will see in Chapter 4, the things that are naturally shared include, in Locke's view, responsibility to God through the moral laws governing how we treat other people. Those moral laws are known to all people (or at least knowable in principle by all people, even if some remain ignorant through their own closed-mindedness) through natural reason. Revelations from God, by contrast, are not naturally shared; they are not even "natural," but supernatural. And government's job is to look after natural things, not supernatural things.

iv. THE METHOD OF REASONABLE FAITH – GOD

When our reason looks to the universe we live in, what does it dis-cover? Locke begins his treatment of this question in Book IV of the *Essay*, laying the foundation of the method by mapping out the basics of reason and faith. He develops that method further in his other writings, where he considers practical questions ranging from how we can confirm whether something is a revelation from God to how we deal with differences in belief that create conflict.

The fundamental thing reason discovers about the universe, in Locke's opinion, is that there is an all-knowing, all-powerful God who created it. Before he even gets to questions like the role of reason and judgment in belief formation, the importance of degrees of assent, or the relationship between reason and faith, the very first thing he has to say about what we know is that we know there is a God.

Locke holds that God's existence can be validated by logic, without relying on any input from the senses, such that we can be absolutely certain of it. He provides a short and informal review of three logical arguments for God's existence – what are traditionally called the "cosmological argument," the "first mover argument" and the "argument from reason."

If anything exists now, Locke argues, then something must always have existed. "Man knows by an intuitive certainty that bare nothing can no more produce any real being, than it can be equal to two right angles." Here Locke is making a reference to the practice of logical proof in geometry. We are accustomed to using intuitive knowledge as a basis of logical reasoning, such as in geometry, where we know by intuition that any two right angles must be equal to each other; in a similar way, we know by intuition that something cannot come out of nothing. If at any time in the past nothing existed, nothing could ever have come into existence. "If, therefore, we know that there is [now] some real being, and that nonentity cannot produce any real being, it is an evident demonstration that from eternity there has been something" (E IV.10.3, 620).

If any events are occurring now, Locke argues, then an eternal omnipotence must always have existed to have set them in motion. "Next, it is evident that what had its being and beginning from another, must also have all that which is in and belongs to its being from another, too. All the powers it has must be owing to, and received from, the same source." So not only does the existence of anything require eternal existence, but any action, motion or power requires an eternal source that produces all such actions, motions, or powers. "This eternal source ... of all being must also be the source and original of all power; and so this eternal being must be also the most powerful" (E IV.10.4, 620).

And if any minds are thinking or perceiving now, Locke argues, then an eternal omniscience must always have existed to endow them with reason and perception. It is "impossible that things wholly void of knowledge and operating blindly, and without any perception, should produce a knowing being ... for it is repugnant to the idea of senseless matter, that it should put into itself sense, perception and knowledge" (E IV.10.5, 620–621).

Since we know simply by reflection within our own minds that something exists, occurs, and thinks, we have all three of these proofs together before we even open our eyes. "If we will suppose nothing first or eternal, matter can never begin to be; if we suppose bare matter without motion [to be] eternal, motion can never begin to be; if we suppose only matter and motion first or eternal, thought can never begin to be" (E IV.10.10, 624). And if you put eternal and unlimited being, power, and mind together, you have an eternal person – God. "From what has been said, it is plain to me [that] we have a more certain knowledge of the existence of a God than of anything our senses have not immediately discovered to us. Nay, I presume I may say that we more certainly know there is a God than that there is anything else without [i.e. outside of] us" (E IV.10.6, 621).

Of course, not everyone acknowledges this knowledge. Or, to put it another way, "we know" does not mean that everyone does know, but simply that everyone can know if he is willing. "When I say we know, I mean there is such a knowledge within our reach which we cannot miss, if we will but apply our minds to that, as we do to several other inquiries" (E IV.10.6, 621).

All these arguments were many centuries old before Locke's time, and Locke is not offering anything his audience hasn't already heard. He does not bother to phrase the arguments with great care, defend them at length, or anticipate objections. Presumably he was aware that these arguments were already being discussed at greater length in many other forums, and any reader interested in hearing more rigorous versions of the arguments or dealing with objections to them could easily find such discussions. At any rate, while Locke's treatment of the certainty of God's existence is emphatic, it is not formal or lengthy.

v.   GOD AND MORAL AUTHORITY

Locke treats it as fairly obvious that an eternal, infinite, omnipotent, omniscient creator God has absolute moral authority. "Having the idea of God and myself, of fear and obedience, I cannot but be sure that God is to be feared and obeyed by me" (E IV.11.13, 638). In other words, as soon as the very concepts we need to perceive it are present to our minds, Locke believes, it is clear to us that God is in charge of the universe.

God is therefore the ultimate standard of right and wrong. God's will is "the only true touchstone of moral rectitude" (E II.28.8, 352). The idea that someone might acknowledge the existence of an eternal, infinite, omnipotent, omniscient creator God and *not* submit to his authority as the absolute standard of right and wrong doesn't seem to have been one Locke took very seriously.

Christian theologians fall into two broad camps on the question of why human beings have a moral obligation to obey God. The debate is complex and many subtleties are lost in any short summary, but a brief overview may still be helpful. One school, the "intellectualists," holds that our moral duties are grounded in God's mind. God knows the good perfectly, while we – made in his image but fallen – know it imperfectly; we should therefore defer to his superior wisdom. The other school, the "voluntarists," holds that our moral duties are grounded in God's will. God made us and we are his creatures; we should therefore obey when he commands.[63]

The difference between the two approaches matters for political philosophy, because it bears on the question of how much and what kind of moral agreement is needed in society. The intellectualist position generally implies that society requires a greater amount of agreement on the content of what is good and bad, but less on the question of where goodness and badness ultimately come from. The voluntarist approach generally implies that society needs less agreement about what is good, but more agreement that "good" is a transcendent standard demanded of us by a higher power.[64]

Locke does not speak at length about the debate between these two positions, but when the subject comes up, he always identifies himself squarely in the voluntarist camp. One of the recurring themes in Locke's works is the need for moral obligation in the foundation of politics, and the impossibility of grounding obligation in anything else but God.

He notes that the two major approaches to ethical theory that exclude the transcendent – ultimately grounding all morality on enlightened self-interest (represented, for Locke, by the thought of Thomas Hobbes) or on the intrinsic dignity of human nature (represented by Aristotle and other ancients) – fail to create obligation (see E I.3.5, 68). Once you have decided that the highest thing in life is to pursue your self-interest or to fulfill the dignity of human nature, a figure like Hobbes or Aristotle may well become your guide. But those who don't think self-interest is the highest thing in life have no obligation to listen to Hobbes, and those who don't think human dignity the highest thing have no obligation to listen to Aristotle.

Political theory must be able to show something in government that makes obedience to it obligatory – not just preferable, since preferences differ from person to person. The problem is, no one can hold up a finite object – whether self-interest or human dignity or anything else – and say that it is obligatory for all people to make that object the highest thing in life. On what grounds do you say that this finite object is mandated rather than some other one?

> The mind has a different relish, as well as the palate; and you will as fruitlessly endeavor to delight all men with riches or glory ... as you would to satisfy all men's hunger with cheese or lobsters. ... Men may choose different things, and yet all choose right, supposing them only like a company of poor insects, whereof some are bees, delighted with flowers, and their sweetness; others, beetles, delighted with other kind of viands. ... Hence it was, I think, that the philosophers of old did in vain enquire whether *summum bonum* [i.e. "the supreme good," the good that contains all others within it] consisted in riches, or bodily delights, or virtue, or contemplation; and they might have as reasonably disputed, whether the best relish were to be found in apples, plums or nuts, and have divided themselves into sects upon it. (E II.21.55, 269–270)

Locke put the same point another way in a later book, where he wrote that when moral philosophy is not grounded in God, it cannot speak with authority. He proposed an experiment: suppose you could construct an exact duplicate of Christian morality by gathering the wisdom of the greatest philosophers in history – "some from Solon and Bias in Greece, others from Tully in Italy, and to complete the work, let Confucius, as far as China, be consulted, and Anacharsis the Scythian, contribute his share." Without God, this would produce only "sayings," not "laws":

What will all this do to give the world a complete morality that may be to mankind the unquestionable rule of life and manners? ... What would this amount to toward being a steady rule, a certain transcript of the law that we are under? Did the saying of Aristippus or Confucius give it an authority? Was Zeno a lawgiver to mankind? If not, what he or any other philosopher delivered was but a saying of his. Mankind might hearken to it or reject it as they pleased, or as it suited their interest, passions, principles or humors. They were under no obligation; the opinion of this or that philosopher was of no authority. (R 243, 172–173)

God, on the other hand, is a source of obligation. And as the only infinite object, God obviously has no rivals – it would always be irrational to prefer anything else to God.

Therefore, seeking God's will is the main business of human life. "Our proper employment lies in those inquiries, and in that sort of knowledge, which is most suited to our natural capacities and carries in it our greatest interest, i.e. the condition of our eternal estate. Hence I think I may conclude that morality is the proper science and business of mankind in general" (E IV.12.11, 646).

Throughout the *Essay*, the knowledge of God is what justifies Locke's focus on the ethics of belief. As we noted in Chapter 2, Locke's concern in the *Essay* is to emphasize our responsibility to regulate our beliefs. It is our duty to God that grounds this responsibility.

Also, the knowledge of God justifies Locke's lack of interest in some of the more traditional areas of focus in epistemology. If there is a God, then we don't need to be very worried about questions like whether our perceptions of the world through the senses are systematically unreliable. God gave us these senses; who are we to doubt them?

Men may find matter sufficient to busy their heads, and employ their hands with variety, delight, and satisfaction, if they will not boldly quarrel with their own constitution, and throw away the blessings their hands are filled with because they are not big enough to grasp everything. ... It will be no excuse to an idle and untoward servant, who would not attend to his business by candlelight, to plead that he had not broad sunshine. The candle that is set up in us shines bright enough for all our purposes. (E I.1.5, 45–46)

vi. THE METHOD OF REASONABLE FAITH – EVIDENCE AND REVELATION

Merely knowing of the existence of God is not sufficient even for religion. What is God like? What does he want from us? Logic alone cannot tell us; we must investigate the world around us to see what evidence we can find to tell us more about our creator.

In his works, Locke builds two methods of discerning God's will. One is the use of natural reason to analyze the world God created, especially the way he constructed human nature, to discern a "natural law" regulating our behavior. This is undertaken in Locke's major political work, the *Two Treatises of Government*, and we will examine it in Chapter 4.

The other is to search the world for evidence of revelation from God. Has God spoken to humanity? This subject comes up indirectly in all of Locke's works, since they all include some measure of biblical analysis. Yet in most cases – the *Two Treatises* and the *Letter Concerning Toleration* being the most notable examples – Locke takes the truth of Christianity and the authenticity of the Bible as God's word for granted, without going into why he believes these things.

One place Locke does take up the question of how we discover revelation in the world is in his 1695 book *The Reasonableness of Christianity as Revealed in the Scriptures*. The book was written partly to a Christian audience, to address controversies about what beliefs were necessary for salvation, but it was also partly for a non-Christian audience – specifically, deists, people who believe in God but do not accept revelation as a way of learning about God. Locke sought to show that it was reasonable to accept revelation and that historic Christianity did not entail any unreasonable beliefs (hence the book's title).

In both the *Essay* and the *Reasonableness*, Locke argues that we can distinguish true revelations from God by the presence of miracles. Only God could cause a miracle to occur, so prophets who work miracles (or whose authenticity is attested by those who do) are trustworthy. Faith accepts truths "upon the credit of the proposer, as coming from God, in some extraordinary way of communication" (E IV.18.2, 689). It is the performance of miracles that give a prophet "credit" as a "proposer" of revealed truth, because only God, "who has the power to change the course of nature," could cause a miracle (E IV.16.13, 667). Thus "miracles ... well attested, do not only find credit themselves, but give it also to other truths which need such confirmation" (E IV.16.13, 667).

Those who do not see the miracles themselves must judge whether miracles occurred by such evidence as eyewitness testimony. As Locke put it in one of his other religious works, "he that believes the history of the facts, puts himself in the place of a spectator."[65] And it is significant that in the *Essay*, Locke points to historical events (he cites Julius Ceasar's victory over Pompey) as prime examples of the kind of thing we can believe in with certainty even though we don't directly witness them, because they are so well attested (E IV.16.8, 662).

This might be called an evidence-based approach to faith. Locke provides a rational reason for faith that works in essentially the same way all our other beliefs work. If we want to know whether a doctor is competent, or a politician is trustworthy, or a friend is loyal, what do we do? Examine the evidence. We should judge whether a prophet really speaks for God in the same way.

But it is important not to overstate the importance of evidence in Locke's system. For Locke, knowing the existence of God comes before the evidence and provides the framework within which we judge the evidence. Historically, arguments over the evidence for miracles have often been framed in terms of examining the evidence about miracles in order to judge whether God exists. From Locke's perspective, this would be putting the cart before the horse. The question of whether a given miracle (such as Jesus rising from the dead) occurred should only be evaluated after we first determine – by logic, not evidence – whether we live in a universe superintended by an omnipotent, and therefore potentially miracle-working, God. If we do, that must naturally shape our expectations for what kind of evidence is sufficient to establish whether a given miracle occurred.[66]

This approach to judging the authenticity of revelation by miracles was not new; it has always been an approach some Christians take.[67] In the *Reasonableness*, to show that this approach does not contradict Christian theology, Locke combs extensively through scripture to demonstrate that it is affirmed there.[68] In doing so, he also implicitly argues against those who take a less evidence-based approach to faith and yet believe in the Bible – in effect, Locke is showing that those who believe the Bible should be following an evidence-based approach.

Locke's works do not engage in a serious review of the evidence for the Christian miracles. He indicates that he believes the evidence establishing that Jesus did rise from the dead, as well as the other Christian miracles, is overwhelming. "The evidence of our savior's mission from heaven is so great, in the multitudes of miracles he did before all sorts of people, that what he delivered cannot but be received as the oracles of God and unquestionable verity" (R 237, 164). But he doesn't go over that evidence. As with the logical arguments for God's existence, this was a subject on which his audience already had a great abundance of information available. The contribution Locke wanted to make was to frame our approach to that information – to keep us focused on the evidence rather than on our religious feelings or traditions as the ultimate basis of our belief.

In addition to judging the authenticity of revelation (based on the evidence of miracles), reason is also necessary to interpret the revelation. Reason is what we use to examine a text and determine its meaning – and sometimes it takes a lot of reasoning to work out the meaning of a difficult text (see E III.9.22–23, 489–490). Thus, we should not be surprised if we find that people sincerely and in good faith disagree about the meaning of many texts, and we should not be "magisterial, positive and imperious, in imposing our own sense and interpretation" of them (E III.9.23, 490). This mention of "imposing" our interpretation of religious texts can only refer to the criminal laws of the day, which punished wrong religious belief as a civil crime.

Thus religion, for Locke, is rational not only in its basis, but in its method. Understanding the content of revelation is the paradigmatic religious activity – it is what gives direction and shape to all the other aspects of religion. And this activity of the understanding, by its nature, requires freedom from coercion.

But, as has already been noted, reason cannot pass judgment on the content of revelation. Once reason has confirmed that a text really is a revelation from God and determined its meaning, reason itself demands that the content must be true. So although Locke's faith is fully rational, it is not rationalism.

vii.   "FAITH IS NOT FAITH WITHOUT BELIEVING" – TOLERATION

Locke wrote extensively on the content of scripture and its implications for theology. Most aspects of these writings aren't directly relevant to his political and social ideas. But one way in which they were deeply relevant was in making the case for religious toleration.

Locke's argument for religious toleration is most fully laid out in his *Letter Concerning Toleration*, written during his exile in Amsterdam after the Exclusion Crisis and first published – in Latin, with the hope of reaching Christians throughout Europe – in 1689. His other works reinforce the case in the *Letter* in various ways.

The *Letter* makes a very aggressive case for toleration by arguing that government's authority is strictly limited to what it calls "civil concernments" – people's lives, liberty, and property (L 5–7, 17). Regulating these civil matters in order to preserve each person's right to his own life, liberty, and property is the only function of government.

So Locke is not simply arguing for less government activity in one area. He is not just saying that when it comes to religion, government should try to take a more hands-off approach. Locke is basing his argument on a fundamental model of what government is for and how it is supposed to operate. What's at stake here is not simply whether government will be relatively strict or relatively permissive when it comes to religious laws, but the much more basic question of what government exists for across the board.

The arguments of the *Letter* are at least as much about Christian theology as they are about political philosophy. Locke begins with a blistering attack on religious laws as fundamentally incompatible with the love of all people that should serve as the Christian standard. If a person is "destitute of charity, meekness, and goodwill in general toward all mankind, even to those that are not Christians, he is certainly yet short of being a true Christian himself. ... It is in vain for any man to usurp the name of Christian without holiness of life, purity of manners, benignity and meekness of spirit" (L 1, 13).

Locke identifies religious persecution as a result of ungodliness and wickedness in the persecutors:

> If the gospel and the apostles may be credited, no man can be a Christian without charity, and without that faith which works, not by force, but by love. Now I appeal to the consciences of those that persecute, torment, destroy and kill other men upon pretense of religion, whether they do it out of friendship to them or no? (L 1, 14)

Support for religious freedom is thus "the chief characteristic mark of the true church" (L 1, 13).

Whereas, Locke asserts, those who are so eager to persecute the errors of others outside their church communions tend to be very lax and permissive when it comes to the moral failures of their own coreligionists:

> For if it be out of a principle of charity, as they pretend, and love to men's souls, that they deprive them of their estates, maim them with corporal punishments, starve and torment them in noisome prisons, and in the end even take away their lives – I say, if all this be done merely to make men Christians and procure their salvation, why then do they suffer whoredom, fraud, malice, and suchlike enormities ... to predominate so much and abound amongst their flocks and people? (L 1, 14)

Locke then offers some more systematic arguments for why government should limit itself to civil concerns. The first is that the government cannot show any basis for authority over faith; neither the Bible nor natural reason establishes such a claim. Nor could people legitimately give government that kind of authority over them even if they chose to do so by consent, because "no man can so far abandon the care of his own salvation as blindly to leave to the choice of any other, whether prince or subject, to prescribe to him what faith and worship he shall embrace" (L 9, 18). This argument connects closely to Locke's more general approach to the nature of government authority, and we will be coming back to it in Chapter 5 in that context.

The second argument is that government has no power to affect faith even if it had the authority to do so. It can punish people, and thus it can change behavior. But it cannot change minds, and in religion, minds are what count. "All the life and power of true religion consist in the inward and full persuasion of the mind, and faith is not faith without believing." And the government's "power consists only in outward force ... and such is the nature of the understanding that it cannot be compelled to the belief of anything by outward force" (L 10, 18).

The third argument is that enforcing faith detaches it from the sincere search for truth. Even if government had both the authority and the means to control faith, how would it serve the interest of truth in religion if we put our rulers in charge of it? "There being but one truth, one way to heaven, what hope is there that more men would be led into it if they had no rule but the religion of the court?" Our rulers are no better positioned to know the truth about God than any other people – and if we put them in charge of our consciences, their "secular interests" are far more likely to guide them than the genuine search for truth. At best, "one country alone would be in the right, and all the rest of the world put under an obligation of following their princes in the ways that lead to destruction." And, making this approach even more absurd, "men would owe their eternal happiness or misery to the places of their nativity" (L 12, 19–20).

However, the underlying idea that ties together all the arguments in the *Letter* is that government doesn't need to, nor does it have authority to, enforce every single moral law without exception. Locke points out that sins like pride, gluttony, and envy aren't punished by civil law even among those who favor religious laws:

> It does not follow that because it is a sin, it ought therefore to be punished by the magistrate. For it does not belong unto the magistrate to make use of his sword in punishing everything, indifferently, that he takes to be a sin against God. Covetousness, uncharitableness, idleness and many other things are sins, by the consent of men, which yet no man ever said were to be punished by the magistrate. The reason is because they are not prejudicial to other men's rights, nor do they break the public peace of societies. (L 54, 42)

Instead, government only needs to enforce the moral laws that are necessary to the preservation of society. As we saw in the Introduction, the fundamental problem of religious toleration is that there is a natural relationship between religion and morality, and there is also a natural relationship between morality and politics. Government needs to be able to enforce the moral laws that define the civil community, such as those forbidding murder and theft. And moral laws, in turn, have their foundation in what people believe about the ultimate nature of the universe.

Locke's most fundamental argument is that disputes over theology aren't the same as disputes over moral laws like the prohibitions against murder and theft. People who don't believe murder is wrong are a threat to society, but religious disagreements don't fall into that category. These disputes may affect our beliefs about moral laws in some areas of life, but they don't affect the particular moral laws that are of concern to politics.

Or, at least, they usually don't. Locke acknowledges that some religious beliefs – such as advocacy of child sacrifice, to take an extreme example – would come into conflict with the moral laws necessary to preserve the civil community. In those cases, toleration must yield to the government's legitimate authority to enforce civil laws.

The general principle is that religious toleration is limited by the community's need to enforce the moral laws governing the civil concerns of life, liberty and property. And the reason for this principle is that toleration itself *is* the enforcement of a moral law governing civil concerns – specifically, the moral law that it is unjust to deny people the equal rights of other citizens simply because of their beliefs. Opposing religious toleration is the same kind of action as murder or theft:

> These ... who attribute unto the faithful, religious and orthodox – that is, in plain terms, unto themselves – any peculiar privilege or power above other mortals in civil concernments; or who upon any pretense of religion do challenge any manner of authority over such as are not associated with them in their ecclesiastical [i.e. church] communion ... What do all these and the like doctrines signify but that they may, and are ready upon any occasion to, seize the government and possess themselves of the estates and fortunes of their fellow subjects; and that they only ask leave to be tolerated by the magistrate so long until they find themselves strong enough to effect it? (L 69, 51)

So Locke sees no conflict between religious toleration and enforcing the moral law – religious toleration is enforcement of the moral law.

Paradoxically, when discussing the limits of religious toleration, Locke actually endorses the criminalization of beliefs that threaten either the civil community or the moral laws on which it is based (see L 68–71, 50–52). His primary example is beliefs that are hostile to religious toleration, but he also includes two other examples: beliefs that require allegiance to a hostile foreign power, and atheism. This position cannot be reconciled with his more fundamental commitment to the idea that civil laws cannot change beliefs. Even if we accept that hostility to religious toleration is a threat to the community, on Locke's own principles we should expect that banning it by law would not be effective.

To those reading it today, Locke's argument that atheism can be criminalized (on grounds that denying God undermines all moral laws, and hence undermines the moral laws on which the civil community is based) seems to be at odds with his arguments for religious toleration. Locke did not perceive it to be so, because Locke grounds the knowledge of God in natural reason rather than revelation. While it does conflict with his stance that criminal laws are not an effective way to respond to intellectual errors, it does not conflict with his broader concept of "religious" toleration – in his opinion, atheism does not even rise to the level of a dispute over religion; it is a dispute over logic.

viii.   THEOLOGY AND TOLERATION

The analysis of the *Letter* intersects with Locke's theology in some of his other works. For example, in the *Reasonableness*, he emphasizes that the "repentance from sin" necessary to salvation is primarily a work of the inner heart, changing our fundamental attitude toward sinful things, and only incidentally about outward actions. This view is presupposed in the distinction Locke draws in the *Letter* between "civil concernments" and matters pertaining to salvation – the *Letter* takes it for granted that the regulation of outward things is not directly related to saving souls.[69]

Another area of overlap is Locke's argument in the *Reasonableness* that all people who turn away (repent) from sin and trust Jesus for their salvation will in fact be saved. The central issue in Christian theology has always been that God is perfectly just and all human beings deserve punishment from him, therefore his punishment of our sin must occur – but Jesus offers us salvation from that punishment and a restoration of our favor with God. The question is how we receive that salvation. Locke pushes hard on this point, arguing that no error of doctrine (other than on the point that Jesus is our savior) will prevent people from being saved so long as they trust Jesus.[70]

This argument is theological rather than political, but it removes the case for having religious laws on many of the matters that religious laws governed. Perhaps most importantly, it implies that

Christians of all types are saved – drawing the fangs from the under-lying conflict in England between Puritans, traditional Anglicans and Catholics, as well as the more basic Protestant v. Catholic conflicts throughout Continental Europe.

Locke picks up this theme in the *Letter*, observing that most of the things religious laws regulate are not necessary for salvation:

> If I be marching on with my utmost vigor in that way which, according to the sacred geography, leads straight to Jerusalem, why am I beaten and ill-used by others because, perhaps, I wear not buskins [a type of boot]; because my hair is not the right cut; because, perhaps, I have not been dipped in the right fashion; because I eat flesh upon the road, or some other food that agrees with my stomach; because I avoid certain by-ways which seem unto me to lead into briars or precipices; because, amongst the several paths that are in the same road, I choose that to walk in which seems to be the straightest and cleanest; because I avoid to keep company with some travelers that are less grave, and others that are more sour, than they ought to be; or, in fine, because I follow a guide that either is, or is not, clothed in white or crowned with a miter? (L 36, 30–31)

But this is not to say that Locke only extends toleration to Christians. While his focus is on the disputes between Christian groups, he also applies the same principles to others. "Neither pagan nor Mahometan [i.e. Muslim] nor Jew should be excluded from the civil rights of the commonwealth because of his religion" (L 77, 56). He notes that a Muslim whose religious beliefs required him to support the Ottoman Empire in its war to conquer Europe could not be tolerated, but this would be because he has put himself in a state of war with the civil community rather than because of his religion as such (see L 70, 51–52). The Ottomans had besieged Vienna in 1683, so when the *Letter* was published in 1689 this was not an abstract or hypothetical issue. Yet Locke makes it clear that the limits of tolera-tion are set by civil rather than religious concerns.[71]

ix. RELIGIOUS FREEDOM AND MODERNITY

The argument for religious toleration in the 1689 *Letter* went well beyond the merely prudential arguments for toleration Locke had advanced in the 1660s. The younger Locke had advocated religious toleration simply on grounds that criminalizing dissent is counter-productive; it only creates more dissent, and makes dissenters more dangerous by making them enemies of the civil order. That argument is still present in the *Letter* (see L 72–75, 52–55) but it is no longer the main focus. Instead, Locke insists that religious toleration is a fundamental right; refraining from religious persecu-tion is one of the fundamental demands of decent behavior.

This fundamentally shifts the ground of the political order. The connection between religion, morality, and politics has been recon-ceptualized. The political order is still fundamentally based on moral law, and moral law is still fundamentally based on religion, just as in earlier political thought. But a clear dividing wall has been constructed between politics and religion. Politics must live off what might be called the cultural capital of religion, in the form of moral order, without directly touching religion itself.

The case of atheism is, of course, a problematic exception – Locke wants politics based on those elements of "religion" that are acces-sible through natural reason. But this exception is small compared with the much larger change in conception his theory requires. That matters pertaining to faith and revelation should have no role in the justifying the state's legitimacy, and hence that the state should have no role in safeguarding orthodox belief, was a position with radical consequences.

The idea that the political order has its roots in natural reason was not, as we have seen, radically new in itself. It had deep roots in medieval thought. What was radically new was the willingness to apply this principle consistently and thoroughly.

Earlier political philosophy had tried to accommodate civil laws compelling religious orthodoxy within the framework of a govern-ment based on natural reason. It was the failure to work out the internal contradictions of this system that led to the wars of religion in the sixteenth and seventeenth centuries. The conception of government as not only rooted in natural reason, but also confined to making laws within the sphere of natural reason, defined the transition from the medieval world to the modern.

CHAPTER 4

LOCKE'S NATURAL LAW

Locke faces a difficult problem in outlining the grounds of political authority. On the one hand, the civil community needs to enforce some moral laws, such as those against murder and theft. And, as we have seen in Chapter 3, Locke thinks that only God can provide an adequate basis for moral obligation, and hence for moral law. Enlightened self-interest, the dignity of human nature, and other proposed alternative frameworks for moral philosophy are only attractive to those who already prefer those things over other things; they cannot show a reason why anyone would be obligated to follow them.

But on the other hand, as we have also seen, Locke believes just as adamantly that matters pertaining to faith are not an appropriate basis for civil laws. Even if we lay aside the question of saving souls (which cannot be done through coercion) and look only at what is needed to preserve the civil community, we cannot build a shared civil community on matters pertaining to faith and revelation. Neither religious traditions nor religious enthusiasms nor even a careful, rational interpretation of the texts of scripture will be voluntarily shared across multiple groups. And if we try to force these things on people who don't voluntarily share them, we undermine everything they stand for.

The political community must therefore find some ground of moral obligation stemming from God but not dependent upon faith – that is, upon revelations from God. The only way out of this dilemma is to build political obligation entirely on what natural reason can tell us about God's will for our behavior.

This is the basic concept behind "natural law," which holds that God has made known to all humanity at least a basic set of moral obligations. The natural law is called natural because it is held to be a part of human nature. Knowing about these obligations is, at least in principle, simply one aspect of being human – although there may be particular individuals who lack this capacity (just as there are particular individuals who lack certain mental or physical capacities) or who are so stubbornly close-minded they have blinded themselves to what they ought to know.

The idea of working out a basis for government in natural reason by identifying a moral law known to all people was far from new in Locke. The concept stretches back to the ancient Greco-Roman philosophers. And the Christian appropriation of this concept is not much older than Christianity itself; it has its roots in the thought of Augustine at the turn of the fifth century. From that time until the twentieth century, natural law was the predominant mode of Christian political philosophy.[72]

But there was a new element in the approach to natural law that emerged among Locke and his contemporaries. It was the view that only the natural law could be politically enforced. Earlier periods had been comfortable with civil enforcement of religious laws alongside laws based on natural reason. But when that model became unsustainable in the religious wars of the sixteenth and seventeenth centuries, the new model that emerged put all the weight of civil government on natural law alone.

This changed the stakes in natural law philosophy. Earlier thinkers working out accounts of natural law knew that their theories did not have to do all the work. Indeed, they knew that all the important bases (do not murder, do not steal, obey the law, etc.) were already covered in revelation, so there was what you might call a redundant failsafe built into the system. If natural law theory wasn't convincing, revelation would do the same job just as well (and vice versa). In effect, there were few functions natural law theory had to fulfill on its own – such as addressing questions of detail that were not specifically settled in scripture, or showing why political laws should be made and enforced by civil rulers rather than the church.

Now, however, with the rise of religious freedom, natural law had to become the foundation of the entire system. Locke had to build an account of natural law that would, on its own, do all the necessary work of justifying civil laws and political institutions.

i.   LOCKE'S EUDAIMONISM – HAPPINESS AND MORALITY

Locke's approach to natural law, like most natural law theories, follows an approach to ethics known as "eudaimonism." This approach closely connects moral law with human nature, such that moral goodness tends to produce a happy and flourishing life.

The approach traces its intellectual lineage back to Plato and Aristotle. In the *Nichomachean Ethics*, Aristotle argues that there is a moral order inherent in human nature, such that those who behave rightly are acting in accordance with their own natures and will therefore have a natural tendency for their lives to flourish – to become *eudaimonia* ("blessed"). Those who act wrongly, by contrast, have a tendency toward ending up wretched and unhappy, because they are at war with their own natures.[73]

Eudaimonism was overwhelmingly the predominant approach in classical Greco-Roman, medieval Christian, and early modern (both Christian and non-Christian) ethical philosophy. One of its greatest exponents was the Roman philosopher Cicero, for whose works Locke had a lifelong admiration and whose ethical thought was deeply influential on him.[74] The introduction of natural-law and eudaimonistic philosophy into Christian thinking was largely a result of Augustine's equally deep admiration for Cicero's works.[75] In spite of the religious implications of the word *eudaimon* ("blessed"), Greco-Roman eudaimonism had been only somewhat religious. But the approach was invested with more serious religious significance when it was taken up by Christian thinkers; as one scholar puts it, eudaimonism "had always been a part of Christian thought" because it provided "additional evidence of man's fallen nature while underscoring the personal quality of God's sovereignty."[76] Not until the rise of Immanuel Kant in the eighteenth century was there a serious, sustained challenge to eudaimonism's dominance over western ethical thought.

The point of eudaimonism is not that any given individual will infallibly be happy as long as he's morally good, no matter what calamities might occur to him. Some eudaimonistic theorists, most notably Plato, do advocate that position. But it is not necessary to believe that to be a eudaimonist, and in fact most eudaimonistic theorists do not rest their theories on that idea. Aristotle, for example, argues that we cannot fully judge whether someone is truly *eudaimonia* until after his death, because whatever blessedness he has, he may lose it.[77] Locke himself is somewhat ambivalent about this question.[78]

The key point, rather, is that morally good actions have a tendency to promote human happiness in general and on the whole. If I find a wallet full of money, returning it to its rightful owner rather than pocketing the cash may or may not make me happier in the short term than keeping the cash would have. But it will certainly make the rightful owner happy! And, in general and on the whole, being the kind of person who returns wallets when he finds them will have a tendency to make me happier in the long run than I would have been if I were the kind of person who kept them. So across multiple people and over longer periods of time, doing the right thing promotes much more happiness.

As Locke comments in the *Essay Concerning Human Understanding*, there is "nothing that so directly and visibly secures and advances the general good of mankind in this world as obedience to the laws" that God "has set them, and nothing that breeds such mischiefs and confusion as the neglect of them" (E II.28.11, 356). God has, "by an inseparable connection, joined virtue and public happiness together; and made the practice thereof necessary to the preservation of society" (E I.3.6, 69).

The justification for this approach is that we were designed by God, and it is clear from his design that behavior and happiness are intimately connected. By reflecting on our own psychology, we discover that the God who made us must care a great deal about our happiness, since he designed us to seek it out. And from reflection on our experience we discover that God has connected happiness to some behaviors and discomfort to others (see E II.7.3, 129). If we want to find out more about the moral plan God had in mind when he made our nature, seeing what makes people happy is a sensible place to look.

ii. EUDAIMONISM AND NATURAL LAW

Eudaimonistic ethics does not imply that whatever makes people happy must be right. The shoe is on the other foot; what is right tends to make people happy. The difference is important because short-term happiness does not always correspond to moral goodness. If we set out to do whatever will make people happy, we might do all sorts of wrong, and in the long term make people both wicked and wretched.

Rather, eudaimonistic ethics looks at what has made people happy over the long term and across large numbers of people to search for evidence of what is right. If a behavior consistently serves to promote the flourishing of human blessedness in every historical period and in every civilization, it is hard to avoid concluding that it is conducive to the moral plan in human nature and thus morally good.

In his *Two Treatises of Government*, Locke marshals evidence from human experience across times and cultures to lay out a general pattern that reveals God's moral plan in human nature. Locke argues that by comparing people across all times and cultures, we can distinguish some things that are always and everywhere appropriate to human nature. This approach is typical of natural law philosophies in all time periods.

An approach that builds on what is universal in humanity seems implausible to many people. Are there really enough things that are universal in humanity? In our own time, cultural particularism – an emphasis on what makes cultures distinct – is much more emphasized than any perspective that sees universal human phenomena. People have been trained to see differences more than similarities.

Cultural particularism was also especially on the rise in Locke's time. In the Middle Ages, the predominance of ethical eudaimonism and natural-law political philosophy served to at least maintain some reminder of universal things. But starting in the fifteenth century, a number of developments had produced a dramatic shift in emphasis. The printing press shifted cultural and intellectual activity from Latin (the universal language in the west) to particular languages like German, French, and English; this divided national cultures from one another. The Reformation and the wars of religion dramatically deepened these divisions. The Ottoman Empire's conquest of Hungary and invasion of eastern Germany, which many feared would lead to the conquest of all Europe, was a sobering reminder of the radical hostility between Christian and Muslim cultures. Perhaps most dramatically of all, the discovery of the "new world" transformed the European conception of the very world in which they lived, revealing that there were whole continents of people who had no connection with their cultural world. Did the Protestant English really have all that much in common, morally speaking, with the Catholic Spaniards whose Armada had tried to conquer them, the Muslim Turks who were now trying to conquer the whole continent, and the unevangelized and uneducated "heathens" in the Americas?

Yet Locke – following the long line of natural law philosophers before and after him – argues that there are clear and important universal patterns in our nature and history. The differences, unsurprisingly, demand our immediate attention much more often than the similarities, because the differences are what threaten us with conflict, engage our curiosity, and so forth. The similarities tend to fade from view. Like an empty sky behind a landscape dotted with interesting features, we don't notice it precisely because it's so large.

iii. THE EVIDENCE OF NATURAL CAPACITIES

To make his case for the natural law, Locke brings three forms of evidence. The first, and most famous, is the design of human beings themselves – the construction of their nature.

Locke observes that God has uniquely endowed human beings with abilities, primarily intellect and will, that allow them to exercise dominion over – that is, use, even to the point of destroying – all the other things in nature. And these abilities have "belonged to the whole species" (T I.30, 24).

The right to exercise dominion must not be taken for granted. Given that God made everything, it all belongs to him and we cannot exercise dominion where he doesn't intend us to. Given that we need to exercise dominion over non-human nature to survive and thrive, it's clear that God meant for us to do so. But no one has that kind of warrant to claim the right to exercise dominion over his fellow humans:

> Men being all the workmanship of one omnipotent and infinitely wise maker; all the servants of one sovereign master, sent into the world by his order and about his business, they are his property, whose workmanship they are, made to last during his, and not one another's pleasure. (T II.6, 117)

Because the abilities that allow human beings to exercise dominion are present in the whole species, it is clear that God did not intend for dominion to be a privilege of the few:

> Being furnished with like faculties, sharing all in one community of nature, there cannot be supposed any such subordination

among us, that may authorize us to destroy one another, as if we were made for one another's use, as the inferior ranks of creatures are for ours. (T II.6, 117)

God has shared the mandate of dominion equally with all people, because he gave them all the same will and intellect, and therefore no one person has the right to exercise dominion over another – to use or destroy him for his own purposes.

One thing that follows from this is that "reason ... teaches all mankind who will but consult it that, being all equal and independent, no one ought to harm another in his life, health, liberty or possessions." Harming other people would be using them – treating them as our property, as objects of dominion. Locke calls this a part of "the law of nature" which "obliges everyone" (T II.6, 117).

Locke makes an exception for cases where we harm others in ways that do not imply we want to treat them as objects of dominion. The most important such exception is where we harm someone in self-defense or in defense of others. Reframed with this exception in mind, the rule not to harm others becomes "force is to be opposed to nothing, but to unjust and unlawful force" (T II.204, 218).

Another thing that follows is that there is no "natural" authority of one person over another. People are by nature politically free and equal. This doesn't mean that political authority cannot be legitimately instituted, it just means that our rulers cannot claim that their authority is inherent in their (or our) nature. We will look more closely at that in Chapter 5.

iv. THE EVIDENCE OF CULTURAL PRACTICES

Locke's second form of evidence is cultural practices. Here he has to be careful, because any one given cultural practice may be corrupt – just because society does something doesn't mean it's right. To ensure that he separates the fundamental design of human nature from things that people just happen to like (which may be evil), Locke distinguishes what he calls "common" practices and "universal" practices.

Just as the things that make an individual happy may not be morally good, because the individual himself may not be morally good, in the same way the practices of any given society at any given time may not be morally good. Citing societies with practices such as cannibalism, Locke writes:

Thus far can the busy mind of man carry him to a brutality below the level of beasts, when he quits his reason, which places him almost equal to the angels. Nor can it be otherwise in a creature whose thoughts are more than the sands and wider than the ocean, where fancy and passion must needs run him into strange courses if reason, which is his only star and compass, be not that [which] he steers by. The imagination is always restless and suggests variety of thoughts; and the will, reason being laid aside, is ready for every extravagant project; and in this state, he that goes furthest out of the way is thought fittest to lead, and is sure of [the] most followers; and when fashion hath once established what folly or craft began, custom makes it sacred, and 'twill be thought impudence or madness to contradict or question it. (T I.58, 42)

Societies err just as much as individuals. When only one person goes wrong, society may correct him, but if a whole group of people all go wrong at the same time, their error becomes self-reinforcing because "fashion" and "custom" establish and nurture it.

Thus, as he explains in another passage, a mere appeal to "common practice" is not a moral justification. The fact that something is a common practice in some particular time and place doesn't speak to whether it's conducive to the plan of human nature. In this passage, one of the issues at stake is the "common practice" in ancient Greece and Rome of taking unwanted babies out into the woods and leaving them to die. Robert Filmer, to whose authoritarian book *Patriarcha* Locke is responding, had argued that this "common practice" establishes that fathers have the rightful power of life and death over their children. Locke replies that infanticide was a "common practice" in ancient Greece and Rome because, in this particular way, ancient Greece and Rome were morally flawed.

But, as Locke goes on to say in this passage, the right of children to inherit their parents' property on their death – another issue at stake between Filmer and Locke – is a reflection of human nature. We conclude this because all, or virtually all, societies in all times and places have practiced it. "Where the practice is universal, 'tis reasonable to think the cause is natural" Locke concludes (T I.88, 63). A universal human practice, not one that happens to be common in a particular society, is an indicator of what really aligns with God's design of human nature.

Locke connects the right to inheritance to the general duty of parents to nurture and care for their children, which is also universally observed among humanity. "For children being by the course of nature born weak and unable to provide for themselves, they have, by the appointment of God himself, who hath thus ordered the course of nature, a right to be nourished and maintained by their parents" (T I.89, 63).

From this and other evidence, Locke draws the moral that it is not enough to refrain from harming people. Human life is positively valuable and we have a duty not only to refrain from harming or destroying it, but to preserve and propagate it.

Locke therefore adds a positive duty to assist others when their preservation is in danger as another part of the natural law. "Everyone, as he is bound to preserve himself and not to quit his station willfully, so by the like reason, when his own preservation comes not in competition, ought he as much as he can to preserve the rest of mankind" (T II.6, 117). This includes a duty to give to others if they are in extreme need (T I.42, 31).

v. THE EVIDENCE OF HISTORICAL PATTERNS

The third form of evidence Locke relies on is historical patterns. We can observe some ways in which people confronted with similar situations always tend to respond in the same way. If these patterns are strong enough, Locke thinks they can give us evidence of God's design in human nature.

Perhaps the most striking example of this is in the final section of the *Two Treatises*, where Locke is defending the right to rebel against tyrannical governments (a topic we will look at more closely in Chapter 6). Locke notes that one of the most frequent objections to the right of rebellion is that telling people they have this right leads them to rebel irresponsibly. People have a natural dislike for being ruled, goes the argument, and can always find plausible excuses to throw off their restraints. Unless they are constantly reminded that they have no right to rebel, they will constantly rebel for minor reasons and cause a great deal of unnecessary bloodshed.

Locke provides three responses, all appealing to the evidence of history. His first response is that "when the people are made miserable and find themselves exposed to the ill usage of arbitrary power," they will rebel whether you tell them they have a right to or not. You can "cry up their governors as much as you will for sons of Jupiter, let them be sacred and divine, descended or authorized from heaven," and "the same will happen." Here Locke is alluding to the history of ancient Rome, where emperors were held to be divine and sons of gods, yet rebellions occurred frequently. Moreover, "he must have lived but a little while in the world who has not seen examples of this in his time; and he must have read very little who cannot produce examples of it in all sorts of governments in the world" (T II.224, 229).

Locke's second response is that the historical record shows that "revolutions happen not upon every little mismanagement in public affairs." Rebellions occur when "a long train of abuses, prevarications and artifices, all tending the same way, make the design [of tyranny] visible to the people" (T II.225, 229).

His third response is that "this doctrine," the right to rebellion, is "the best fence against rebellion." Far from increasing the frequency of rebellions, promoting the idea of a right to rebellion actually decreases their frequency. This is because it reminds "those who are in power" of "the danger and injustice" of abusing their power (T II.226, 229–230). Where the people are ready to rebel, the rulers are less likely to give them a reason.

At first, these responses only make an empirical point. Critics of the right to rebellion make a claim about the historical record, and Locke argues that the historical facts don't bear them out.

But Locke then uses this review of the historical record to make a moral point. "If the innocent, honest man must quietly quit all he has, for peace's sake, to him who will lay violent hands upon it," he writes, "I desire it may be considered, what kind of peace there will be in the world, which consists only in violence and rapine, and which is to be maintained only for the benefit of robbers and oppressors" (T II.228, 231). "Are the people to be blamed if they have the sense of rational creatures, and can think of things no otherwise than as they find and feel them?" (T II.230, 232).

The moral point behind these observations is that a pattern of human behavior which is consistent through history is a reflection of God's design. Locke argues that people in every age have endured great mismanagement without rebelling, but have rebelled whenever a ruler's particular pattern of misbehavior reveals a deliberate design of tyranny. This happens to be precisely the moral rule Locke lays down in his theory of rebellion – that rebellion is not justified by mere mismanagement, however gross and extreme, but is justified when the ruler's behavior makes it clear that he has an intentional plan to tyrannize.

Locke did not begin by deriving the right to rebellion from historical observations. He argues that it is a necessary consequence of the natural law. But once he has derived it in principle, he goes to the historical evidence to confirm that it is, in fact, conducive to human nature in practice. If it were not, he could not confidently offer it as a natural law.

vi.   LOCKE'S NATURAL LAW – CLASSICAL, MEDIEVAL, AND MODERN

Locke's account of the natural law combines the influences of both classical Roman and medieval Christian natural law philosophies. But it is also, in another way, distinctively modern.

The most obvious sign of classical influence, which comes to Locke especially from Cicero, is Locke's relatively basic model of human psychology. Most of the earlier Christian thinkers tended to have relatively complicated ideas about what motivated people. These thinkers were, in their turn, following the tradition of the ancient Greeks, especially Aristotle. But Locke, following many of the ancient Romans as well as a minority of medieval Christian writers, thinks that people are fairly simple – they pursue things that give them enjoyment and avoid what they find unpleasant.[79]

The medieval Christian influence on Locke is obviously the God-centeredness of his account of natural law. Locke is not interested in human happiness for its own sake; he's only interested in it insofar as it helps him figure out God's law. When he finds evidence of God's law that has nothing to do with human happiness – for example when he analyzes our natural capacities – he's just as willing to use that. The only thing that matters is to figure out what God wants.

But Locke's natural law theory is distinctively modern in that it does not seek to figure out the entirety of God's law. Instead, Locke is only interested in the portion of the law that is so crystal clear in natural reason that it can be politically enforced without dividing society.

With extreme religious divisions producing catastrophic social fragmentation in seventeenth-century England, Locke needs to find a natural law that everyone will agree on. For everyone to agree on it, it not only needs to be based on natural reason, but it needs to be confined only to that portion of the moral law that is so obvious everyone will readily agree to it. Otherwise he'll just have traded one socially divisive set of rules for another.

As a result, unlike the much more lengthy moral codes produced by previous natural law thinkers in both the classical and medieval periods, Locke's natural law has only one provision: that human life ought to be preserved, and violence should only be used to counteract the unjust violence of others.

Locke argues that his law of nature is so obvious, those who refuse to acknowledge it are essentially acting like animals – and may be treated as such:

> One may destroy a man who makes war upon him ... for the same reason that he may kill a wolf or a lion: because such men are not under the ties of the common law of reason [and] have no other rule but that of force and violence, and so may be treated as beasts of prey, those dangerous and noxious creatures that will be sure to destroy him whenever he falls into their power. (T II.16, 123)

The one provision in Locke's natural law does have many applications, and these applications confront us with some tricky problems, as we will see in the next two chapters. It is not a simple provision to carry out. But it is much simpler than previous versions of the natural law had been – which is one reason subsequent thinkers tended to follow Locke's lead, and narrower accounts of the natural law became a distinctive quality of political thought in the modern era.

CHAPTER 5

LOCKE'S NATURAL RIGHTS

"The great question," writes Locke in the *Two Treatises of Government*, "which in all ages has disturbed mankind, and brought on them the greatest part of those mischiefs which have ruined cities, depopulated countries, and disordered the peace of the world, has been, not whether there should be power in the world, nor whence it came, but who should have it" (T I.106, 73). Political philosophy is, at bottom, seeking a method of identification. We all know someone is going to have power. But how do we figure out who ought to? That is what "the greatest part" of the world's troubles have always been fought over.

England in the 1680s had more than its share of such troubles. The Exclusion Crisis had torn the country apart and threatened to touch off a new civil war. Locke wrote the *Two Treatises* precisely to justify the Whigs' turn to violent resistance against the king, because in their view he had forfeited his right to power.

This issue of who has the right to rule takes us to the heart of political philosophy: political authority. The key to politics is not power, but right. The mere exercise of power doesn't define politics; a mugging is an assertion of power, but not of political power. What defines politics is when people claim to have the right to power – not just rule but the right to rule. That right is political authority. Politics is what happens when someone says, not merely, "I will do things to people without their consent," but also, "and I am right to do so."

Locke's answer to this problem combines a radical commitment to the natural equality and freedom of all human beings with a solid affirmation of both the necessity and the rightness of establishing a government with a strong mandate to rule. A large part of the popularity of Locke's political philosophy can be attributed to the way he combines commitments to both freedom and authority, to equality and rulership.

i. WHO'S IN CHARGE? MERE FORCE VS. AUTHORITY

Once he has established the content of the natural law – human life is to be preserved as much as possible – he comes to the question of enforcement. If this is God's law, how does God want it put into action, and by whom?

Locke takes it as given that if the natural law is God's law, somebody must have the right to enforce it. "The law of nature would, as all other laws that concern men in this world, be in vain, if there were nobody that ... had a power to execute that law" (T II.7, 118). So the question becomes who has this power.

Earlier in the *Two Treatises*, Locke has framed this as the decisive problem of political philosophy. A theory of how power should be used "would be of no behoof for the settling of order and establishment of a government in its exercise and use amongst men, unless there were a way also taught how to know the person to whom it belonged to have this power" (T I.81, 59). Locke makes these remarks in the course of replying to the absolute monarchist Robert Filmer, who had claimed (in his 1680 book *Patriarcha*) that kings ruled with a power descended from Adam's original dominion over the entire world; one of Locke's most devastating replies is to point out that even if we wanted to derive authority from this source, we have no way to know who, among all the people of the world, is Adam's true heir.

More generally, Locke rejects the view (not uncommon among amateur political philosophers) that government has title to rule simply because someone must. We need not just a justification that someone must rule, but a justification of the particular people who have a right to do so.

Otherwise power would be its own justification. And in that case, there would be no politics at all. There would only be the exercise of brute force. And if there is nothing to ruling but brute force, as soon as anyone has the chance to seize power there is no reason not to do so – once you seize power, you become the rightful ruler, because power is its own justification. If that were the case, "he that has force is without more ado to be obeyed, and crowns and scepters would become the inheritance only of violence and rapine" (T I.81, 59–60).

Politics does involve the use of force, but what distinguishes the world of politics from a world of mere brute force is inducing people to submit to it willingly (even if they're not necessarily happy about it) by arguing that obedience to that power is obligatory. This requires the giving of reasons, which must specifically distinguish the particular rulers as rightful authorities. People obey when they perceive this distinction, and "that cannot be the reason of my obedience, which I know not to be so; much less can that be a reason of my obedience which nobody at all can know to be so" (I T.124, 85). "Nobody in conscience can be obliged to obedience, but when it be resolved" who has a right to be obeyed, but people will obey when justifications are shown (T I.105, 73).

Thus the key characteristic of political authority is rule by consent. (As we will see in more detail below, "rule by consent" is not the same thing as democracy.) The consent of the people is obtained by showing them that their obedience to a particular ruler is morally obligatory.

The contrast between consent and force frames the entire argument of the *Two Treatises*. There are only two ways to organize social behavior – persuade people to cooperate by choice, or intimidate them into cooperating by force. For Locke, rule by consent is the foundation of law and authority, while rule by force is the foundation of tyranny and slavery.

Filmer did not think he was arguing for slavery, of course, but for the unconditional right of the government to rule. Locke believes that's a distinction without a difference.[80]

ii. NATURAL EQUALITY AND NATURAL RIGHTS

The obvious next step is to search for any evidence that God has anointed anyone with the authority to enforce the natural law. There are only two places to look for such evidence: nature and revelation.

Locke spends much more time examining revelation than nature on this quesiton. The entire first treatise in the *Two Treatises* is devoted to scriptural interpretation. There, Locke sets up his reading of the Bible as a counterpoint to Filmer's biblical argument for absolute monarchism based on "divine right." The key distinction between natural law and divine right theories is whether the king rules because the community consents to his rule, or because he has an immediate mandate from God.

Today, the theory of divine right is the subject of much historical confusion. It was not a holdover from the Middle Ages. The medieval period was dominated by natural law philosophy and the theory of rule by the consent of the community, not divine right.[81] The ascendance of divine right theory, especially in England, occurred in the sixteenth and seventeenth centuries as a result of the Reformation and the wars of religion. It was facilitated by Henry VIII's consolidation of power in the throne (see Chapter 1) and it, in turn, continued to facilitate further royal consolidation of power.[82]

Thus when Locke takes on the theory of divine right in the name of rule by consent, he does not see himself as knocking down the dead husk of medieval authoritarianism to inaugurate a bold new era of rule by consent. Rather, he sees himself as restoring the ancient theory of rule by consent against a radical new pretender who has recently overthrown it and usurped its place.

The *First Treatise of Government* is not much read today, because there are few people left who believe anything like what Filmer believed. Why bother reading the refutation of something nobody now believes? But there is much more going on in the *First Treatise* than just a refutation of Filmer.

Locke's purpose in the *First Treatise* is not merely to show that Filmer's attempt to derive political authority from the Bible is wrong. It is to show that all attempts to derive political authority from the Bible are wrong. The argument of the *First Treatise* involves extensive parsing of biblical text and we need not review it here. The key point is that, in addition to a specific case against Filmer, arguing that he misread the Bible, the *First Treatise* makes a general case that no particular person can claim to have a right to rule based on the biblical text. The Bible affirms that there ought to be a civil ruler, but it does not answer the question of who should rule.[83]

Locke's argument against Filmer in the *First Treatise* draws extensively on the same approach to the problems of interpreting language that he laid out in the *Essay Concerning Human Understanding*. Again and again, Locke asserts that the fundamental difference between his theory and Filmer's is that Filmer does not seek out the meaning of the text that the author would have intended it to have. In all other contexts, using a text as if it had a meaning that the speaker didn't intend is called twisting people's words; and we should apply the same rule to the words in the Bible as we do to all other words. "God, I believe, speaks differently from men, because he speaks with more truth, and more certainty; but ... I do not think he speaks differently from them, in crossing the rules of language in use amongst them" (T I.46, 34). Otherwise there would be no point to God's speaking at all.[84]

Having shown that no one can claim political authority from revelation, Locke turns to nature. As we saw in Chapter 4, Locke argues that in God's design of human nature, the relevant point for this question is that the capacity to have dominion over – to use and destroy – other things, meaning especially the capacities of intellect and will, are present in the entire human species. The need to exercise dominion – the need for food, clothing, etc. – is also diffused through the species. Every human being is therefore constructed by God to be an exerciser of dominion. This implies that no human being is made to be an object of dominion.

By nature, then, the human race is in a state of freedom and equality:

> [The] state all men are naturally in ... is a state of perfect freedom to order their actions, and dispose of their possessions and persons, as they think fit, within the bounds of the law of nature, without asking leave or depending upon the will of any other man. A state also of equality, wherein all the power and jurisdiction is reciprocal, no one having more than another; there being nothing more evident than that creatures of the same species and rank, promiscuously born to all the same advantages of nature and the use of the same faculties, should also be equal one amongst another, without subordination or subjection. (T II.4, 116)

If no one has the right to use or destroy anyone else for his own ends, then no one has a natural political authority over others.

So someone must have authority to enforce the natural law, since it is God's law and cannot be void. Yet no particular person has a specific mandate to such authority, either from nature or revelation.

Locke takes these premises and makes a bold deduction. If someone must have authority to enforce the natural law, yet no particular person has a specific mandate for it, it must follow that – at least by nature – everyone has that authority equally:

> That all men may be restrained from invading others' rights and from doing hurt to one another, and the law of nature be observed,

which willeth the peace and preservation of all mankind, the execution of the law of nature is ... put into every man's hands, whereby everyone has a right to punish the transgressions of that law to such a degree as may hinder its violation. (T II.7, 118)

Anyone who sees a wrong being committed may enforce the natural law, either intervening to stop the wrong or punishing the wrong-doer afterwards.

Locke acknowledges that to some, this will seem like a bizarre conclusion, but it really isn't. "I doubt not but this will seem a very strange doctrine to some men; but before they condemn it, I desire them to resolve me, by what right any prince or state can put to death, or punish, an alien for any crime he commits in their country" (T II.9, 119). If the law drew its authority ultimately and finally from merely human conventions, it would not extend to foreigners, who don't participate in those conventions. Yet everyone seems to agree that governments can enforce their laws against foreigners who enter their territories. The law must therefore have a ground of authority that reaches further back than human conventions – to a ground in the divine construction of human nature.

If there is anyone, anywhere, who is born without naturally possessing the right to protect himself against being forcibly used by others, that person is a slave. And we know from the construction of human nature that no one is born to be a slave, because by God's design everyone is born possessing the same "made for dominion" nature.

This is the idea of "natural rights" – the idea that we are all born with rights. In Locke, as in most ethical theories, a "right" is simply the inverse of a duty. If I have a duty not to steal things from you, you have a right not to have your things stolen by me. The idea of natural rights is simply that the construction of human nature, reflecting God's design, implies that there are moral limits to how we can rightfully treat people. We have a natural duty not to treat people as property, and therefore people have a natural right not to be treated that way.

iii.   THE STATE OF NATURE

Of course, none of this corresponds to what we actually see going on in the world around us. Everywhere we look, we see power structures – people ruling and being ruled. And we see not just power but political authority; people don't just wield power and have it wielded over them, but they believe this power is rightful.

If people are free and equal by nature, then all political authority structures must be artificial rather than natural. If political authority is not equally shared, but instead some people have authority over others, this state of affairs goes beyond humanity's natural state. This is what Locke calls a state of "civil society," or just "society" or "community."

The question becomes, can the existence of artificial political authority structures be justified? God made us all free and equal. Can we justify changing that situation and constructing a different structure?

This is why Locke famously turns to the idea of a "state of nature." The function of the state of nature in the *Two Treatises* is to find out what the world would be like without artificial political authority structures. If we tore down all our political institutions and lived with no political authority whatsoever other than the authority to enforce the natural law that we all possess by nature, what would things be like?

Like much of Locke's thought, this idea has roots in medieval political philosophy. Locke's concept of what the state of nature is does not differ very much from, say, William of Ockham's in the fourteenth century.[85]

The state of nature is not a past historical event. It is not an account of something that happened a long time ago, either at the start of human history or in some undefined, legendary past.[86]

The state of nature takes place in the present as well as in the past. It is the state people are in at any time when they have no obligations to anyone other than those that derive directly from human nature – the obligations we have to each other simply because we are human. States of nature occur all the time. Every human being is in a state of nature at birth (see T II.119, 176). Nations are always in a state of nature relative to one another – this is the point Locke is making in the argument, quoted above, that governments can punish foreigners because all people have, by nature, the authority to enforce the natural law. You yourself can experience the state of nature any time you wish; simply renounce your citizenship, get on a boat and sail out into international waters.

Locke uses the concept of the state of nature to ask a provocative question: what would happen if the entire world all did that at the same time? What if everyone were simultaneously in a state of nature relative to everyone else?

This is a thought experiment designed to clarify the basis of artificial authority structures. Locke addresses the question of why we have an obligation to obey artificial authorities by asking what life would be like without them.

iv. LIFE IN THE STATE OF NATURE

We would, of course, all be free and equal if we were all simultaneously in the state of nature – that's what makes it a state of nature. However, our lives would be structured by the law of nature. Unlike Hobbes, Locke believes that the moral law is a fundamental part of human nature; even in the absence of rulers and society, people would still believe in right and wrong.[87]

Drawing on the construction of human nature and our knowledge of typical human behavior, Locke reviews the ways in which the law of nature would shape our lives in the state of nature. He focuses, in turn, on three major phenomena.

First, he says, we would get into lots of fights. After the chapter called "Of the State of Nature," his next chapter is called "Of the State of War." By "state of war" Locke doesn't mean international wars, but any state of enmity in which someone has a consistent desire to destroy another.

If everyone in the state of nature has the right to enforce the natural law with punishments, we can expect people to try to punish each other every time they have a grievance (real or imagined) against someone. That will put a lot of people at war with each other.

Far from being a sunny optimist about human nature, Locke believes people are naturally selfish. They are "biased by their interest" and "partial to themselves" (T II.124–125, 178–179). The natural selfishness of human beings is a theme that runs consistently through the *Two Treatises*.[88]

Locke stresses that the state of nature is not just a constant state of war all the time and with everybody – which was Hobbes's view. Yet Locke does think violent conflict would happen with some regularity in the state of nature.

Second, to preserve our own lives, we would need to work – in order to eat, have shelter, and fulfill our other biological needs. We would need to exercise that dominion over nature which (as we have seen) Locke sees as central to the special value and dignity of human life. We would need to appropriate plants and animals out of the realm of nature for food, appropriate materials for clothing and shelter, and so forth.

In other words, property ownership would occur in the state of nature. Survival is mandated by the law of nature, so whatever is necessary to survival is protected by the law of nature. We cannot eat, or otherwise make use of things, without appropriating them to ourselves privately. The apple has to become exclusively mine before it can nourish me, since two people cannot both eat the same apple (see T II.26, 127–128).

Locke argues that people's work is the basis of property. No one has any special claim to ownership over nature; the whole world was given to us all. Yet natural things must become privately owned before we can use them for survival. Therefore, in the state of nature we must have a right to take them and use them. So things would become privately owned when people appropriated them out of the common stock of nature – which happens through labor:

> He that is nourished by the acorns he picked under an oak, or the apples he gathered from the trees in the wood, has certainly appropriated them to himself. Nobody can deny but the nourishment is his. I ask, then, when did they begin to be his? When he digested? Or when he ate? Or when he boiled? Or when he brought them home? Or when he picked them up? And 'tis plain, if the first gathering made them not his, nothing else could. That labor put a distinction between them and [what is] common [to all people]. That added something to them more than nature, the common mother of all, had done; and so they became his private right. (T II.28, 128)

That property is a natural rather than artificial institution was an issue of some importance. It was connected to taxation, which was central to the dispute between Parliament and the king. The parliamentarians and their supporters pointed out that under the English constitution as it had developed up to that point, taxes could only be raised with Parliament's consent. The monarchists said practices such as the king seeking Parliament's consent were merely prudential, and could never ultimately take away the king's final authority.

Locke emphasizes that because property rights are natural and pre-political, not an artificial creation of government, rulers cannot just arbitrarily make any rules they want regarding people's property. Civil laws governing property exist primarily to protect the natural rights of individuals, not to serve the interests of the rulers. Locke argues that if a political constitution contains rules safeguarding people's interest in their property – such as limits on the taxation power – those rules should be treated as fundamental mandates and not mere prudential practices that can be changed at will (see T II.140, 187; and II.142, 188).

Third, there would be families in the state of nature. Procreation is obviously a part of human nature, and is also commanded by the natural law (see T I.59, 43). The family, for Locke, exists in nature to carry out that design by caring for children (see T II.55, 141).

Locke spends considerable time discussing parental authority over children. Filmer and others had derived political authority by analogy to parental authority, so Locke is at pains to show how radically different these two forms of authority are. "The father's power of commanding extends no further than the minority of his children, and to a degree only fit for the discipline and government of that age" (T II.74, 151). In addition, it does not include the "legislative power of life and death," which is the essential distinguishing mark of political power (see T II.86, 157). And parental authority is shared equally by husband and wife, whereas political authority must create a final judge (see T II.52, 140).

V. ARE SOCIETIES FORMED BY FORCE OR CONSENT?

The big question is, given this situation in the state of nature, what would morally justify the creation of a political authority structure? As we have observed, for Locke there are only two ways to organize social action – by force or by choice. Locke considers both alternatives.

In his discussion of violence in the state of nature, Locke considers whether such conflicts could ever lead to the creation of a political authority structure. Some thinkers in Locke's day traced the sovereignty of the English kings back to the victory of William the Conqueror in 1066 (see T II.177, 207). And the view that all governments ultimately owe their existence to the use of force has always had some advocates in political philosophy.

But Locke argues that violent conflict, while it may lead people to take their enemies captive as slaves, cannot by itself create the political authority necessary to make them subjects. The problem is not that war is never justified – sometimes it is. If people are unjustly attacked they have a right to fight back, and if they fight back they might win. So a just conquest is possible.

But even if the act of conquest is just, something else is necessary to create a society. The most that a just conquest can lead to is slavery, and slavery is "nothing else but the state of war continued between a lawful conqueror and a captive" (T II.24, 126). And a state of war, far from being a state of civil society, is precisely the *opposite* of a state of civil society. Moreover, as Locke comments later in the *Two Treatises*, even if the capture of an aggressor in a just war is justified, holding his children or other noncombatants as captives is not, since they have done no wrong. Even if a just conquest could create some kind of political jurisdiction over the conquered, that jurisdiction could not extend to a whole nation of people over time (see T II.182–196, 208–215).

Since force is incapable of creating civil society, it follows that if civil society were created, it must be created by consent. This is not the same thing as democracy, and in fact it doesn't even imply that democracy is a preferable form of government. It only means that government exists because people acknowledge its legitimacy and submit willingly, not because it rules through mere force and fear.

Of course, not every individual consents to every act of government at every moment; using force is part of governing. The very nature of the act – agreeing to create a society and a government – implies this. The thief who gets caught does not consent to go to jail; he goes because he is forced.

Instead, rule by consent means that the legitimacy of government arises from the consent of the members of the community to be ruled by that government. The members of the community have all given their consent to be ruled – Locke argues that this is what it means to be a member of the community in the first place. Those who refuse to consent to the government are excluding themselves from the community.

This theory of consent is subject to a number of problems; the most important of these is the problem of establishing that people do in fact consent. Consent theory implies – and Locke explicitly affirms – that people are not born as members of the community.

Because people are by nature free and equal, they are free and equal when they are born. Only when they give their consent do they become members of the community, and thus obligated to obey its authority (see T II.119, 176).

Perhaps most people give their consent explicitly at some point or other – actions like voting or obtaining a driver's license may be taken as explicit acknowledgments of the government's rightful jurisdiction. Yet if we catch a person committing a crime, we obviously don't stop to ask whether that person has ever voted or otherwise explicitly consented to the laws before we arrest him.

Locke, like most consent theorists, argues that any adult who chooses to remain in a country and live there rather than leave it has consented – implicitly or "tacitly," even if not explicitly – to be ruled by its laws. "Every man, that hath any possession or enjoyment of any part of the dominions of any government, doth thereby give his tacit consent, and is as far forth obliged to obedience to the laws of that government during such enjoyment, as anyone under it; whether this, his possession, be of land to him and his heirs forever, or a lodging for only a week, or whether it be barely traveling freely on the highway" (T II.119, 176). Only explicit consent can make a person a member of society, but this implicit or tacit consent is all that is needed to legitimately enforce the law. "Submitting to the laws of any country, living quietly, and enjoying the privileges and protection of them makes not a man a member of that society; this is only a local protection and homage" (T II.121, 177).

The theory of tacit consent is subject to a number of objections. Is it reasonable to expect people to undertake the burden of leaving the country as the price of not giving their consent? And where will they go without having to face the same problem elsewhere?

Locke considers these questions, but only briefly, and without much attention to the objections that might be raised to the concept of tacit consent. As we have seen in Chapter 3, his epistemology of religion and his theological writings simply skip over a number of important concerns that were already widely discussed by other authors. Locke also treats the complexities of tacit consent theory in a superficial way, suggesting that he knew these issues had been hashed out many times before by other writers and anyone who wanted to follow those disputes could look them up elsewhere. Locke's concern in the *Two Treatises* is to adjudicate the dispute between rule by force or rule by consent, and his central contention is that rule by force must be illegitimate on any possible considera-tion of the question. It would follow that some kind of theory of rule by consent must be the right approach. Working out the details of how rule by consent works in practice is something the *Two Treatises* simply aren't concerned with doing.

vi. WHY CREATE A SOCIETY?

Locke's job, as he sees it, is to show that it would be reasonable under the law of nature for people in a state of nature to consent to civil society. If he can show that, it would follow that the continued existence of civil society – the political authority structures we see all around us – would also be justified. If it would be reasonable for people in the state of nature to consent to the creation of civil society, it would also be reasonable for us to consent to maintain it.

But would it be consistent with the natural law for people to consent to give up their natural freedom? What would motivate such a decision?

Locke addresses these questions by going into more detail about the causes of violent conflict. Of the major phenomena in the state of nature that he has outlined, violent conflict is obviously the one that poses a problem – a problem that might be solved by the crea-tion of civil society.

The most fundamental problem with the state of nature is that people's moral judgment is biased in their own favor. They may know the natural law perfectly well in the abstract, but when they want to do something wrong, they never have any problem finding some specious excuse for why doing that particular thing wouldn't be wrong. "Though the law of nature be plain and intelligible to all rational creatures; yet men, being biased by their interest, as well as ignorant for want of study of it, are not apt to allow of it as a law binding to them in the application of it to their particular cases" (T II.124, 178).

But they go overboard in the other direction when it comes to how other people treat them – they perceive wrongs where none exist, and even in cases where they were really wronged they use excessive severity. "Men being partial to themselves, passion and revenge is very apt to carry them too far, and with too much heat, in their own cases; as well as negligence and unconcernedness to make them too remiss in other men's" (T II.125, 179).[89]

Note that the problem Locke is pointing out is not only, or even primarily, dealing with deliberate crime – with people who intentionally lie, steal and murder. Much more frequently, people get into disputes where each partly sincerely believes himself to be in the right. Because we each see the world biased in our own favor, we tend to judge our own behavior as morally right regardless of whether it really is, and to judge our neighbors' behavior as morally wrong when they do things we happen to dislike.

Also note that the motivation to do something about this problem is not simply and solely that we don't like having a lot of violent conflict. That is one motivation, to be sure. But another is the sincere desire to see justice done fairly. We know we're not good at judging our own cases – "no one should be a judge in his own case" is a maxim everyone agrees with – so we have a moral as well as a prudential reason to seek out a better system.

There's no way to deal with this problem as long as we're in the state of nature, because in that state there's no escape from the responsibility of passing moral judgment on your own case. "Thus mankind, notwithstanding all the privileges of the state of nature, being but in an ill condition while they are in it, are quickly driven into society" (T II.127, 179).

Because he spends so much time talking about the state of nature, many people interpret Locke as believing that humanity is not "naturally social," in contrast to Aristotle's famous statement "man is by nature a political animal."[90] In fact, Locke's theory shows the opposite – that if it should ever happen that human beings existed without society, they would have to create it.

Particular political structures and institutions are artificial. The king of England is not king by nature, he's king because people agree to treat him as king. If everyone decided to stop treating him that way, he wouldn't be king – as Charles I found out in the English Civil War.

Yet although political structures are artificial, the need for them is natural. That's the paradox of politics: we know that our political institutions are artificial, yet they're not optional or arbitrary. They are there because they serve the needs of our nature.

vii. JUSTICE AND POWER – THE NEUTRAL JUDGE

To escape the troubles of poor moral judgment and violence in the state of nature, we need a neutral judge – an enforcer of the natural law to whom we can bring our disagreements to settle them peacefully. We agree to create society for the purpose of setting up such a judge. Society, once created, establishes a government to rule it.

What makes the neutral judge able to perform its function is that it possesses the moral authority to rule. People agree that they are obligated to abide by its decisions even in cases where they disagree with those decisions. The freedom "of doing whatsoever he thought fit for the preservation of himself and the rest of mankind, he gives up to be regulated by laws made by the society, so far forth as the preservation of himself and the rest of that society shall require," and "the power of punishing he wholly gives up" (T II.129–130, 180).

This surrender of the right to moral judgment is what the whole act of creating society is all about. We know that we're not good at judging our own cases, so we bind ourselves in advance to submit to the judgment of another in our own cases rather than following our own opinion. Otherwise, "what appearance would there be of any compact? What new engagement, if he were no further tied by any decrees of the society than he himself thought fit, and did actually consent to?" (T II.97, 164)

So the function of government is not simply to put force behind the natural law in order to ensure that justice is done. Much more important is government's role as the authoritative judge who settles disputes over what justice requires. Government's defining function is not to exercise power, but to decide what is the fair way power ought to be exercised in each case. Actually exercising the power is a function of secondary importance. It is justice, not power, that defines political communities.

The form of government – democracy, republic, oligarchy, monarchy, etc. – is determined by each society according to what will work best in its circumstances (see T II.132–133, 181–182). Thus, even forms of government that appear to be inconsistent with rule by consent, such as the forms of tribal patriarchy that prevail in primitive societies, are actually consistent with it. Critics of consent theory argue that if government were only legitimate by consent, primitive governments would be democratic rather than patriarchal. Locke replies that, under the conditions that prevail in primitive society, tribal patriarchy is the form of government that makes the most sense – it is the best way to preserve the tribe under those circumstances. Thus, people in those conditions consent to be ruled in that way (see T II.105–112, 167–173).[91]

Because the fundamental purpose of government is to apply the natural law, its most basic function is to make laws. The legislative function is therefore the real heart and foundation of any government (see T II.132, 165 and II.134, 182–183). If the legislative function is held by a different body than other functions such as the executive function, then the legislature is the supreme branch. "In all cases, whilst the government persists, the legislative is the supreme power. For what can give laws to another, must needs be superior to him" (T II.150, 191).

This does not mean that a constitution could not legitimately give some powers to the executive apart from the legislature. It does not even mean that the executive cannot depart from the law in emergencies or other exceptional cases (see T II.159–168, 197–202).

What it does mean, at a minimum, is that the executive has no right to abolish the legislature and set himself up to rule without it (see T II.155, 194). And this, of course, brings us back to the original purpose of the *Two Treatises*. Parliament attempted to exclude James from the throne, and Charles II responded by attempting to abolish Parliament. The *Two Treatises* was written to defend the parliamentary cause.

Of course, neither Charles nor James was persuaded by Whig arguments of this kind. And they had the power to force their way upon Parliament and the nation. The next question, then – the question that lies at the heart of the *Two Treatises* – is what Englishmen could legitimately do to resist the executive's aspirations to absolute rule. Could they take up arms against their own king? We turn to this question in the next chapter.

CHAPTER 6

LOCKE'S REBELLION

In the history of political philosophy, one of the oldest arguments is over whether subjects have a right to rebel against their rulers if the rulers become (by some standard) tyrannical. The standard philosophical argument against rebellion is that the whole point of having a government in the first place is that there must be a final authority who judges all disputes, and to whose judgment everybody must submit even when they disagree with it. If you're going to give people the right to overthrow the government when they don't like what it does, why did you create a government in the first place? To have government with a right to rebellion is not much different in principle from having no government. And, the finishing flourish usually goes, if you look at the history of societies that believed in the right to rebellion, such as in ancient Rome, you'll find that it's also not much different in practice – constant riots and rebellions keep reducing the state to anarchy.

The *Second Treatise* of the *Two Treatises of Government* was written primarily to answer this philosophical argument, just as the *First Treatise* was written to answer the scriptural argument that the Bible unconditionally authorizes the rule of all existing governments. Locke turns the argument against rebellion on its head. In fact, he argues, it is government without the right to rebellion, not government with the right to rebellion, that is not much different – either in principle or in practice – from anarchy. Locke even turns the appeal to ancient Rome on its head: ancient Rome didn't have frequent rebellions because they talked so much about a right to rebellion; rather, they talked so much about the right to rebellion because they frequently found themselves suffering under unbearable tyrannies, and constantly found themselves left with no reasonable alternative but to rebel.

In 1680s England, the argument over the right to rebel was deeply entangled with religious conflict. Both Parliament's fear of unchecked tyranny by the king and the king's fear of self-willed and lawless rebellion by Parliament grew out of England's experience of the wars of religion. Hatred and distrust stemming from religious differences had driven it down the road to chaos, violence, and civil war many times in the previous 150 years. So it was not just that a religious conflict – whether Parliament had the right to exclude Roman Catholics from the throne – was the immediate cause of the Exclusion Crisis. This was just the latest in a long line of such crises.

Locke's argument for a right to rebellion is framed in general terms, so that it could apply to any kind of dispute, not just a dispute over religion. But it was disputes over religion that in fact drove Locke to examine the question in the first place.

This connection to religion is important because of the crucial role of moral law in Locke's approach to rebellion. Locke argues that there must be a right to rebellion because all human beings, including rulers, must be subject – in practice and not just in theory – to that particular type of moral law called the "natural law." That is just inherent in what the natural law is – an absolute moral law laid down for all humanity by God.

So in the *Two Treatises* we see the same architecture of religion, morality, and politics that we see in the *Letter Concerning Toleration*. On the one hand, differences over the content of revelation (which first and foremost meant differences between Puritans, traditional Anglicans, and Roman Catholics) are not relevant civil authority. It's wrong to treat some people as second-class citizens because of where they stand on such questions. On the other hand, the only basis of enforcing any civil law at all is its grounding in moral law. There can be no authority without an obligation to obey; no obligation without a moral law that transcends human preferences; and no moral law that transcends human preferences without God (see Chapter 3). The only way to reconcile these competing imperatives is by establishing God's moral law through natural reason – that is, to know the natural law (see Chapter 4). This provides a basis for authority that can be universally recognized (because it appeals to grounds that are shared across competing faith-groups) and is universally obligatory (because God ordained the natural law to be known and binding on everybody).

i. WHAT JUST HAPPENED HERE? INTERPRETING
THE EXCLUSION CRISIS

As we have seen in Chapter 1, these were not abstract, ivory-tower issues for Locke. Charles II, and then James II after him, were claiming to have absolute authority to rule directly from God. And they were making aggressive use of the claim. They shut down competing sources of authority – including, ultimately, the elimination of Parliament itself – so that they would possess all power; their word literally was the law. And they didn't hesitate to use that power to destroy their enemies; those who opposed their aspiration to absolute rule, or who merely did business with or expressed sympathy for those who did, were put through a rigged trial and then jailed, ruined or executed.

The basic question of the *Two Treatises* is how we interpret this conflict. One way to frame it would be to say that the parliamentarians just didn't want to submit to the rightful king. On one level they may have feared abuses of power, but these fears owed more to their hated for Roman Catholics than to any real danger signs. So they committed a series of increasingly brazen acts of treason to overthrow the rightful king. On this reading, Charles's and James's efforts to suppress their enemies may be seen as overzealous and sometimes abusive – ironically lending some after-the-fact credibility to the parliamentarians' accusations of tyranny. But their efforts were basically directed at a good cause: stopping a treasonous criminal conspiracy.

That, of course, is not how Locke and the parliamentarians saw it. On their view, the tyrannical ambitions of Charles and James came first. In the 1670s, perceiving that Charles had designs to take away their liberties, they began with peaceful resistance within the political system. But as Charles got more and more out of control in the late 1670s and early 1680s, they were increasingly forced to resist by any means necessary. Charles had started a war against his own people, later carried on by James. And actions that would normally be criminal, like deceit and killing, can be positively praiseworthy if they're committed in a war for a just cause.

Which interpretation is right? A key issue for deciding that question concerns the claim to absolute authority itself. Charles and James both announced their claim to have an absolute and unlimited right to rule however they saw fit, recognizing no limits on their power other than their duty to obey God – according to their own opinions of what God wanted from them.

This kind of claim was, historically, relatively new. It was not completely unprecedented, but it had previously been unusual. Traditionally, kings had typically recognized limits on their power. Now, with the consolidation of power in the English throne after Henry VIII, kings were more and more making this type of unlimited claim to power.[92]

The parliamentarians viewed this claim, simply by itself, as strong evidence that their liberties were in danger. And the danger they saw as inherent in the absolutist claim became a lens through which they interpreted every action taken by the king. A single action perceived as an abuse of power might not, by itself, call the fundamental legitimacy of the king into question. But in the context of a claim to absolute authority, every single action by the king was much more likely to be perceived as an abuse of power, and every single perceived abuse of power took on a much larger and deeper significance. If the king abusively executed a person, it was not just that one person's life at stake, but the whole question of whether England would be a free country or a tyranny.

Locke wrote the *Two Treatises* during the Exclusion Crisis, but he published it in 1689, after the whole conflict was resolved and the victory of the parliamentary cause was secured. So while his motive for writing it may have been to affect the outcome of the crisis, he must have had a different motive for publishing it. That motive was to affect the historical memory of the nation – to establish a particular interpretation of the events that had just occurred in order to help the English people draw the right lessons from them.

The primary lesson he wanted people to draw was that the crisis had not fundamentally been caused by abusive behavior from Charles and James. It had fundamentally been caused by the claim they made to have a right to absolute and unlimited authority. Even to make such a claim is to destroy the foundations of civil society, which are grounded in the moral laws of justice (the natural law) and not in any power structure. By definition there can only be one absolute authority, so if the will of the ruler is absolute, then the laws of justice are not absolute. And the laws of justice are nothing at all if they are not absolute; that's part of what it means to call them the laws of justice.

Establishing this interpretation would have meant more than just arguing against the partisans of the overthrown monarchs. Even among the parliamentarians, the meaning of their victory was inter-preted in different ways. The danger, from Locke's perspective, was that the whole crisis would be chalked up to the unusually abusive behavior of a couple of especially bad kings. No deep philosophical issues need be raised on this view – the problem was simply that these kings had refused to behave according to English conventions and traditions defining the boundaries of their behavior.

Against this tendency toward traditionalism, Locke was anxious to establish that the problem was a matter of fundamental moral philosophy. The laws of justice are the only absolute ground of political authority. Traditions, like the will of the monarch, should serve these laws, not rule in their stead.[93]

ii. A BRIEF PRE-HISTORY OF THE RIGHT TO REBELLION

For as long as there have been governments, there have been rebellions. Motives for rebellion have never been lacking. The selfishness of those in power leads to oppression and exploitation, which creates a desire to resist; the selfishness of those out of power constantly tempts them to seize power if the opportunity should arise.

The idea that rebellion can be justified is almost as old as political philosophy itself. In ancient Greece, to kill a tyrant was considered a heroic act. Aristotle, although he does not examine the question directly, seems to endorse this view at least indirectly.[94]

With the rise of Rome, the right to rebellion came to be formally and systematically defended. Cicero, Locke's favorite moral philoso-pher, was the doctrine's most influential defender. He argued that the political community is defined not by governments but by justice – the only thing that makes a group of people more than just a group of people is that they share something, and the thing that makes a political community is a shared commitment to justice. A tyrant, who rules in open defiance of any commitment to justice, therefore destroys the political community. "Whenever I behold a tyrant," says the hero of Cicero's dialogue *On the Republic*, "I know that the social constitution must be, not merely vicious and corrupt ... but in strict truth, no social constitution at all."[95] Since the political community itself is destroyed by tyranny, rebellion against tyrants is not a threat to the political community, but rather vital to its survival.

This line of argument was deeply influential on Christian politi-cal philosophy. The first extended and systematic work of Christian political philosophy, *The City of God*, was produced in the early fifth century by Augustine, who was (like Locke) a lifelong fan of Cicero. While Augustine does not take up the question of a right to rebellion in that work, he introduces all the basic concepts of Cicero's political philosophy. Thereafter, Christians in the west influenced by Augustine (which is almost a redundancy) found Cicero's conclusions on the right to rebellion plausible. Throughout the Middle Ages, government by the consent of the governed and the right to rebellion were the predominant mode of Christian political thought.[96]

Another older argument for rebellion is that if political authority is absolute, then might makes right. Absolutism holds that the ruler's authority is not derived from anything outside himself (such as the natural law or the consent of the community). This implies that all rulers are legitimate simply because they rule; if power is not based on something outside itself, then power is self-justifying. Thus, even the rule of someone who seizes power through deception or murder must be obeyed – a system that creates some very powerful perverse incentives. As Locke puts it, on these premises "he that has force is without more ado to be obeyed, and crowns and scepters would become the inheritance only of violence and rapine" (T I.81, 59–60).

For Christians, one of the most common ways of phrasing this argument was that absolute and unconditional government authority would remove the distinction between slaves and political subjects. All subjects would be slaves if rulers had unlimited power. This argument had been crucial for Christians because it allowed them to ground their case in the Bible. The text of the Bible clearly distinguishes between political subjects who are or are not slaves, which implies that subjection to political authority is not the same thing as slavery. Scripture presupposes that there is such a thing as a "free subject," as distinct from an enslaved subject. Therefore (for the Bible-believing Christian) there must be such a thing. And therefore government authority cannot be unlimited.

The *Two Treatises* is consistently shaped by this approach to the subject. "Slavery" is even the first word of the book. "Slavery is so vile and miserable an estate of man," goes the opening line, "and so directly opposite to the generous temper and courage of our nation, that 'tis hardly to be conceived that an Englishman, much less a gentleman, should plead for it" (T I.1, 5). As we have seen in Chapter 5, one of the bedrock commitments of the *Two Treatises* is the contrast between force and consent. On the political level, this manifests itself as the difference between free subjects and slaves. The subject of slavery comes up again and again throughout the *Two Treatises*, and this conceptual connection between slavery and the king's claim to absolute authority is always the reason.[97]

Another point that is important to Christians (and thus to Locke) for biblical reasons is Cicero's argument that a tyrannical government ceases to be a government at all. This has biblical importance because the Bible commands Christians to obey government.

iii. REBELLION TAKES CENTER STAGE

But not all the arguments were old. Dramatically new issues were surrounding the right to rebellion. Locke was part of a larger struggle in seventeenth-century England to come to grips with the new situation and provide a new response.

Earlier thinking about the right to revolution had taken it for granted that it would not usually be difficult to distinguish a tyrant from a legitimate ruler. If someone seized power by deception or murder, such usurpation was (at least implicitly) tyrannous. Likewise, if someone ruled by arbitrary force, killing and oppressing with impunity and for no discernable legitimate purpose, that was tyranny. Discerning the difference between such obviously tyrannical practices and the normal exercise of political power (even with all the mistakes and lesser abuses that typically occur in any government) was not a difficult problem.

The wars of religion over the previous 150 years had obliterated this easy assumption. It had always been taken for granted that the political community would have a shared religion, and hence that the ruler must share that religion to be legitimate. But after the Reformation, the assumption of a shared faith was removed. No matter who was in power, some large portion of the population regarded that person's faith – and therefore his or her claim to political authority – as illegitimate. Unrest, rioting and rebellions resulted.

Distinguishing the difference between legitimate and illegitimate governments was suddenly a complex question. Rulers could no longer rely on a default presumption that they had the right to rule. Carefully crafted and widely persuasive arguments were needed to establish the legitimacy of governments – and to restrain the tendency toward violence among both the rulers and the ruled.

The Exclusion Crisis is a case in point. Could Parliament legitimately exclude a person from succession to the throne? If so, was Roman Catholicism a legitimate ground for such an exclusion? Could the king legitimately prevent Parliament from meeting to vote on such legislation? Could he go so far as to abolish Parliament to prevent it? And at what point do disagreements over these questions become grounds for violent resistance?

Political philosophy in earlier periods had never delved far into the deep philosophical questions implied by the right to rebellion. There had been no need. But now, the need was urgent. The only way to remove the constant danger of violence and civil war was to develop an account of how we distinguish ordinary political disagreements, ordinary cases of mistakes and mismanagement, and even ordinary cases of abuse of power, from genuine tyranny. How can we know where to draw that line?

iv. SOCIETY AND GOVERNMENT

A detailed map of where the right to rebellion begins is really a map of where the right to government ends. And to find out where government authority ends, we have to understand where it comes from. So a map where the right to government ends ultimately requires a map to where the right to government begins.

We have seen in Chapter 5 why Locke thinks it would be reasonable for people to create a government if they didn't already have one – because without government, each person's bias in his or her own favor warps our moral judgment and creates excessive violent conflict. And since a shared authority cannot be created by force – which can compel people to obey through fear but cannot create a moral obligation to obey – it must be created through consent. The next question is: once people had determined this, how would they create a government?

The first key point Locke wants us to grasp here is that there is a clear distinction between a civil society (or just "society" or "community") on the one hand, and a government on the other (see T II.132, 181 and II.211, 222). If neither society nor government existed, people would first come together and create a society, then society would create government. This must be the case because the act of creating a government for a people presupposes that those people already have a binding obligation to give up their natural equality to an authority structure. Such an obligation can only arise by consent, as we saw in Chapter 5, so people must voluntarily submit to an obligation to obey before government can be created. But they cannot submit to the government itself before that government exists, so there must be something else that people submit to before government is created – namely, the community.

> Men being, as has been said, by nature all free, equal and independent, no one can be put out of this state and subjected to the political power of another without his own consent. The only way whereby anyone divests himself of his natural liberty and puts on the bonds of civil society is by agreeing with other men to join and unite into a community for their comfortable, safe and peaceable living one amongst another, in a secure enjoyment of their properties and a greater security against those who are not of it. (T II.95, 163)

Locke does not pay much attention to the exact process by which people in the state of nature could come together and create a society, and then that society could create a government. He notes that since society could only be created by consent, every individual would have to consent separately to become a member of the new society. And since all individuals at this point would still have their natural equality, as no authority structures had been created, the only mechanism by which a new society could choose a government would be by majority vote. Among equals, there would be no basis for giving any one person more power than another (T II.96–98, 163–164).

Recall from Chapter 5 that the state of nature Locke envisions is a hypothetical thought experiment. Locke is arguing that if we had no government, we would have no reasonable alternative but to create one. Therefore, it is reasonable, at least in general, for us to maintain the governments we see in the world around us, rather than reject their authority.

In describing the process for creating governments, he highlights the distinction between society and government. If we didn't have a government and had to create one, Locke argues, something like the process he's describing – first individuals form a society, then society forms a government – would be the only way to do it. Therefore, the distinction between society and government is necessary.

This matters to our practical obligations. In the actual world we live in, we shouldn't treat government as if it were the only thing we had a responsibility to. We have an even higher responsibility to the political community, from which the government derives its existence. Usually, of course, our duty to society is fulfilled by obeying the government. But if the two are distinct, it is conceivable that in some cases they will come into conflict. And if the government and the community are ever at war with one another, we must know where our ultimate loyalty should lie.

v. CONSENT AND RESPONSIBILITY – AUTHORITY AS A TRUST

This distinction between society and government is crucial because it implies that government holds its authority in trust from the community. Discussing his view that the legislature is the heart of any government (see Chapter 5), Locke draws a crucial distinction. Although the legislature is the supreme power of the government, it is only supreme over the government, not over society. Rather, it is the other way around; the community is supreme over the legislative: "The legislative being only a fiduciary power [i.e. power held in trust] to act for certain ends, there remains still in the people a supreme power to remove or alter the legislative when they find the legislative act[ing] contrary to the trust reposed in them" (T II.149, 191).

It was not disputed in Locke's time that all forms of authority are held in trust. The question was, in trust from whom? Theories of absolutism and divine right held that the king received his authority directly from God, and thus held his power in trust from God and was accountable to God – but not to anyone here on earth – for how he used it.

The traditional medieval view also held that authority comes to the ruler from God, but indirectly rather than directly. On this view, government receives its authority in trust from the community, which in turn had received it in trust from God. The king is therefore responsible for how he uses his power not only to God, but also to the community.

Locke's version of this argument is more characteristically modern because of the role of the individual. He emphasizes not only that government gets its authority from God indirectly, though the community, but also that the community, in turn, had received its authority not directly from God but indirectly, from its individual members. This increased emphasis on the origin of the community in the consent of its members is the basis of the greatly increased concern for individual rights in modern philosophy.

Because authority originates in the moral law, it only extends to use for good purposes. Authority to do wrong is a contradiction in terms. And in particular, because authority is held in trust, it can only legitimately extend to use for the good of those over whom it is held. If authority is held in trust from the community, it only covers the use of power for the good of the community. Locke even defines "tyranny" as "making use of the power anyone has in his hands, not for the good of those who are under it, but for his own private separate advantage" (T II.199, 216).

And if authority is held in trust, it follows that the trust can be forfeited:

> All power given with trust for the attaining [of] an end being limited by that end, whenever that end is manifestly neglected or opposed, the trust must necessarily be forfeited, and the power devolve into the hands of those that gave it. ... For no man or society of men hav[e] a power to deliver up their preservation, or consequently the means of it, to the absolute will and arbitrary dominion of another; [therefore] whenever anyone shall go about to bring them into such a slavish condition, they will always have the right to preserve what they have not a power to part with; and to rid themselves of those who invade this fundamental, sacred, and unalterable law of self-preservation, for which they entered into society. (T II.149, 191)

Because the holding of power in trust from the community is what defines a government, when that government forfeits its trust, it is dissolved. There is no more government at all; there may still be a tyrant who calls himself a ruler, but "government" properly speaking has ceased to exist. There could be no such thing as a tyrannical government, since "government" is defined by its holding and using political authority in trust from the community for its benefit. Tyranny is the opposite of government. "Whosoever, in authority, exceeds the power given him by the law, and makes use of the force he has under his command to compass that upon the subject which the law allows not, ceases in that to be a magistrate; and [because he is] acting without authority, may be opposed, as any other man who by force invades the right of another" (T II.202, 217–218).

One way to sum up this whole argument is to say that if a gang of criminals started calling itself "the government" and forcibly eliminated all rivals to its power, that by itself would not create an obligation for us to obey it. Criminals are not transformed into governments simply by calling themselves "the government." If they exercise power for their own sake rather than to do the proper job of governing, then they never really stopped being just a gang of criminals. From this, it follows that if an existing government actually abandons the job of governing and starts behaving exactly like a band of criminals, it ceases to be a government and becomes a gang of criminals.

vi. TRUST ISSUES

However, at this point we are still left with the question of when, specifically, government's trust is forfeited. It cannot be that every single wrong act by a government justifies rebellion. After all, Locke has already confirmed that it's natural for people to exercise bad moral judgment, because of their bias in their own favor. That's the whole justification for creating government in the first place. So we have to expect that even after government is created, it will show poor judgment in some number of cases. Expecting perfect judgment from government would be unreasonable if the original justification for government is that human beings exercise moral judgment imperfectly.

This implies that there must be a line, somewhere, between ordinary government failures and tyrannical actions that imply the forfeiture of the government's trust. So we are left with the question of where to draw that line. What standard can be justified?

Moreover, the principle that human beings exercise moral judgment imperfectly should make us wary of trusting our own judgment when we think we have reasons to rebel. What appears to me to be an oppressive and tyrannical act by government may only appear that way to me because I'm biased in some way.

Locke has already rejected the conclusion that because we exercise judgment imperfectly, we can never be sure that rebellion is justified. The very act of creating a government, he argues, involves making certain moral commitments. This implies that our moral judgment is not totally useless; if we can know enough to know that we are obligated to obey government, we can know enough to know when our obligation to obey is at an end.

But the problem of imperfect moral judgment obviously must impose limits on the right to rebel, just as it imposes limits everywhere else. Recall two of the consequences of this problem we saw in Chapter 5. First, because moral judgment is imperfect, people find themselves compelled to have governments. "Mankind, notwithstanding all the privileges of the state of nature, being but in an ill condition while they are in it, are quickly driven into society" (T II.127, 179). Second, because moral judgment is imperfect, people who claim the right to rule us must be able to justify that claim with a very clear and convincing case. "Nobody in conscience can be obliged to obedience, but when it be resolved" who has a right to be obeyed (T I.105, 73).

In the same way, because moral judgment is imperfect, those who consider rebellion had better be extremely careful to ensure that their cause is justified. Those who rebel in any but the most certain cases will be held accountable for their reckless behavior at the Last Judgment:

> He that appeals to heaven [i.e. rebels against tyranny] must be sure he has right on his side; and a right, too, that is worth the trouble and cost of the appeal, as he will answer at a tribunal that cannot be deceived, and will be sure to retribute to everyone according to the mischiefs he hath created to his fellow subjects – that is, any part of mankind. (T II.176, 206)

There is one type of case that satisfies all these concerns and establishes beyond doubt that government's trust has been forfeited. That is when the ruler is not even trying to govern fairly, but is deliberately and intentionally using his power for his own selfish purposes. It is a matter of first principles that a ruler cannot be performing the function of a government if he isn't even trying to perform those functions. The fundamental dividing line between tolerable levels of misused power and intolerable tyranny is in the heart and mind of the ruler himself.

The obvious question that arises next is, how can we know when an intentional design of tyranny is present? For Locke, the key to exercising good judgment in politics, as in religion, is to start by getting first principles straight, and then follow the evidence.

One misuse of power cannot, by itself, establish a sustained intention of tyranny. "Revolutions happen not upon every little mismanagement in public affairs," writes Locke. "Great mistakes in the ruling part, many wrong and inconvenient laws, and all the slips of human frailty will be borne by the people, without mutiny or murmur" (T II.225, 229).

However, a long series of abuses can establish that the ruler is misusing power deliberately, especially if the abuses fit into a consistent pattern: "If a long train of abuses, prevarications and artifices, all tending the same way, make the design [of tyranny] visible to the people, and they cannot but feel what they lie under and see wither they are going, 'tis not to be wondered that they should then rouse themselves" (T II.225, 229).

Thus, on Locke's view, the older philosophers were right to proceed on the assumption that tyranny was something obvious. They were just mistaken in basing their definitions of tyranny on particular kinds of oppressive actions such as usurpation of office or exercising power in contradiction to well established laws. The real seat of tyranny is inside the tyrant himself; it is the tyrant's intention to tyrannize. This intention, when it is really present, is not hard to recognize in his actions. "And are the people to be blamed, if they have the sense of rational creatures, and can think of things no[t] otherwise than as they find and feel them?" (T II.230, 232)

vii. NO ESCAPE FROM RESPONSIBILITY

In the end, what the right to rebellion really means is that our delegation of moral judgment to government is not total. We must give up our right to judge disputes for ourselves on a day-to-day basis. But we cannot give up that right totally and finally. There is a residual responsibility for judgment in every individual that is irreducible.

Locke argues that maintaining this level of responsibility which we cannot delegate to government is inherent in the act of delegation itself. Government only exists because we delegate to it most of our responsibility for moral judgment. But the one thing we cannot delegate responsibility for is the act of delegation itself. Responsibility begins not with government, but with us; therefore, when the delegation itself comes into question, we are responsible for justifying it – or else repudiating it.

This, according to Locke, is simply how God has designed human moral responsibility. The very basis of moral responsibility is that we are God's creatures; this implies that we can never ultimately and completely abandon our moral responsibility. The basis of freedom and equality is the moral law that human life must be preserved; therefore, I can never ultimately escape my responsibility to look after my own preservation and that of others. "A man, not having the power of his own life, cannot, by compact or his own consent, enslave himself to anyone, nor put himself under the absolute, arbitrary power of another to take away his life when he pleases" (T II.23, 126). Revolution is what happens when we must fall back on this ultimate, undelegateable level of responsibility.

Locke repeatedly describes revolution – and, indeed, all violence involving a dispute over justice – as an "appeal to heaven" (e.g. T II.21, 125; II.168, 210; II.176, 206; and II.241–242, 240). This is because the basis of revolutions, for Locke, is the permanent, unchangeable fact that all human beings are responsible to God. The ruler is supposed to serve as the shared, neutral judge in disputes over justice. When the dispute itself involves the ruler, as when the community rises up against a tyrant, there can be no such judge. And "where there is no judge on earth, the appeal lies to God in heaven" (T II.21, 125).

This is not a theory of trial by combat; Locke is not implying that God will give victory to the just cause. Rather, he is saying that violent conflicts occur where people believe they are in the right, and are not willing to abandon their cause because they are responsible to God. They are "appealing to heaven" because they are proclaiming that they believe their cause is just and that God wants them to defend it.

Locke also justifies his characterization of any violent dispute over justice as an "appeal to heaven" by pointing to the biblical example of Jephtha (see T I.163, 109–110; II.21, 125; II.109, 170; and II.176, 206). In Judges 11, the Israelites are threatened with attack by a neighboring nation, the Ammonites, who claim that the Israelites have wronged them. Jephtha, leader of the Israelites, writes a letter to the Ammonites explaining why the Israelites have done them no wrong. But since the Ammonites are going to invade anyway, he concludes (in Judges 11:27): "The Lord the judge be judge this day between the children of Israel and the children of Ammon." Since there is no judge on earth between the Israelites and the Ammonites, they appeal to God to judge the rightness of their cause.

viii.   THE *TWO TREATISES* AND THE DECLARATION OF INDEPENDENCE

The same philosophy of rebellion we find in Locke was widely influential in colonial America and profoundly shaped the American revolution. It is probably impossible to say with certainty how much the American revolutionaries were shaped by Locke, as opposed to other sources with similar ideas. On the one hand, many of the same earlier books that influenced Locke, from Cicero's *On the Republic* to Samuel Rutherford's 1644 *Lex Rex*, were influential on the American founders. On the other hand, Locke was himself influential on figures like Jonathan Edwards and William Blackstone, who were in turn influential on the American founders. Who is to say to what extent the American founders drank from the same wells Locke drank from, and to what extent they drank from the wells he dug?[98]

But if the lines of influence are indistinct, the outcome is as clear as the sun in the sky. The Declaration of Independence shows how indistinguishable the political philosophy of the American revolution is from the political philosophy of Locke's *Two Treatises*:

> We hold these truths to be self-evident, that all men are created equal, that they are endowed by their creator with certain unalienable rights, that among these are life, liberty and the pursuit of happiness; that to secure these rights, governments are instituted among men, deriving their just powers from the consent of the governed; that whenever any form of government becomes destructive of these ends, it is the right of the people to alter or to abolish it, and to institute new government, laying its foundation on such principles and organizing its powers in such form, as to them shall seem most likely to effect their safety and happiness. Prudence, indeed, will dictate that governments long established should not be changed for light and transient causes; and accordingly all experience hath shown that mankind are more disposed to suffer, while evils are sufferable, than to right

themselves by abolishing the forms to which they are accustomed. But when a long train of abuses and usurpations, pursuing invariably the same object, evinces a design to reduce them under absolute despotism, it is their right, it is their duty, to throw off such government, and to provide new guards for their future security.

It is an old observation that the line about how it is "self-evident that all men are created equal" and "endowed by their creator" with "unalienable rights" to "life, liberty, and the pursuit of happiness" echoes Locke's conception of the natural law: "Reason, which is that law [of nature], teaches all mankind who will but consult it that being all equal and independent, no one ought to harm another in his life, liberty or possessions" (T II.6, 117).

But in fact the entire passage quoted above – the key passage of the Declaration – mirrors the *Two Treatises* perfectly. Governments are instituted by consent, to secure natural rights; when government becomes destructive of those rights, the people may alter or abolish it; people will suffer great evils rather than rebel; but when it is clear that the abuses are intentional, they will and should rebel.

Consider the question of how Locke and the Declaration define when we have a right to rebel. This must be the most important distinguishing feature of a revolutionary philosophy. When is rebellion authorized? Here is the Declaration: "when a long train of abuses and usurpations, pursuing invariably the same object, evinces a design to reduce them under absolute despotism." And here is Locke: "if a long train of abuses, prevarications, and artifices, all tending the same way, make the design [of tyranny] visible to the people." The criterion to be established – a deliberate "design" of tyranny – and the evidence by which we establish it are alike identical. The overwhelming bulk of the Declaration is devoted to reciting a list of grievances against the king. The purpose of this list, as the Declaration itself states, is not simply to show the wrongs done to the colonists but to establish "a history of repeated injuries and usurpations all having in direct object the establishment of an absolute tyranny over these states."

The founders' deviations from Locke – such as Thomas Jefferson's romantic phrase "pursuit of happiness" standing in for Locke's more concrete term "property" – may not be completely trivial. But these variations in phrasing pale, if not to insignificance then almost that far, when compared to the nearly identical structure of the philosophical framework and the basic argument.

It is interesting to note that during the siege of Boston in the winter of 1775–1776, warships commissioned by George Washington bore flags that declared, in large black letters on a white background, "AN APPEAL TO HEAVEN." The flag was adopted by the Massachusetts Navy in April 1776.[99]

ix. THE PARADOX OF POLITICS

The Lockean approach to the right to rebellion does not ultimately eliminate the problem of flawed moral judgment. People may well abuse the right to rebellion by making flawed judgments about when there is sufficient evidence to conclude that deliberate tyranny is occurring. Locke may argue that such abuses are much more rare and much less serious than the abuses of power that occur when the right to rebellion is not affirmed (see L II.224–226, 229–230). But it remains the case that Locke is only minimizing, not actually solving, the problem of violent conflict.

This reflects Locke's firm commitment to two seemingly paradoxical principles. On the one hand, human nature is radically flawed, such that people will always have a broad tendency to exercise moral judgment imperfectly. On the other hand, people nonetheless do know right from wrong well enough to be responsible to God for obeying the natural law – and therefore people can never ultimately surrender their responsibility for judging matters like whether their rulers are governors or tyrants.

The tension between our moral responsibility and our tendency toward selfish bias is inherent in human nature and can never be escaped. For this reason, there can be no perfectionism in politics, no hope for removing all prospects for violence. As long as we remain human, the problems imbedded in human nature will continue to be with us.

The alternative to living with this paradox would be to deny one of its premises. We could deny that the tendency toward selfish bias is radically ingrained in our nature. This might imply an aristocratic approach to politics, in which those few who are well educated and enlightened enough to rise above petty selfishness are entrusted with power. In its purest form, this is the approach we find in most of the classical Greco-Roman philosophers. Or we could deny that anyone has any ultimately reliable moral knowledge at all – that people are not naturally moral, but are artificially made moral by their participation in society. This approach, championed by Thomas Hobbes, implies political absolutism because it removes all possible moral grounds for individual liberty.

From the Lockean perspective, these choices represent naiveté on the one hand, and cynicism on the other. Real-life experience does not bear out the naïve expectation that giving power to an enlightened few will lead to more enlightened government. Quite the contrary – the more you give people unaccountable power, the more corrupt they become. "He that thinks absolute power purifies men's bloods, and corrects the baseness of human nature, need read but the history of this or any other age to be convinced of the contrary" (T II.91, 160).

And as for the cynics, if they took their cynicism seriously, they wouldn't be writing political philosophy in the first place. They would simply conclude that might makes right, and whatever anyone wants to do is OK. Only a moral law that precedes or transcends society itself and is known to all people simply because they are people can give us a standard against which political action can be criticized. Locke writes that without such a law, "all government in the world is the product only of force and violence, and ... men live together by no other rule but that of beasts, where the strongest carries it" (T II.1, 115).

Ultimately, it is not because of their education or environment that people are persistently selfish (although these things may exacerbate their selfishness). People are ultimately biased toward selfishness simply because they're people. On the other hand, while a selfish bias in applying the moral law to particular cases is part of being human, reliable knowledge of the moral law in general is also part of being human. While this may present us with a difficult paradox in our politics, it's a paradox we have to live with.

CONCLUSION

Summarizing Locke's influence and importance is a daunting task. Probably no one has come closer to providing a concise summary than the scholar who wrote:

> John Locke is the most influential philosopher of modern times. ... Locke's influence reaches far beyond the limits of what has since his time become recognized as the professional discipline of philosophy. His influence in the history of thought, on the way we think about ourselves and our relations to the world we live in, to God, nature and society, has been immense. His great message was to set us free from the burden of tradition and authority, both in theology and knowledge, by showing that the entire grounds of our right conduct in the world can be secured by the experience we may gain by the innate faculties and powers we were born with. God "commands what reason does" are the words that best reveal the tenor and unity of Locke's thought.[100]

If he had only written about epistemology, or only about theology and the philosophy of religion, or only about political philosophy, he would be one of the giants of intellectual history. Having radically transformed all three of these fields simultaneously – and not just among scholars and intellectuals but even more dramatically among the population at large, such that political and social institutions have been widely reshaped according to his thinking – he is a giant among the giants.

i. CLEARING THE RUBBISH – LOCKE'S EPISTEMOLOGICAL LEGACY

Through his epistemology, he led a great turning away from approaches that sought to base our beliefs on complex and speculative metaphysical systems. Locke did not reject all metaphysics, but he argued that the beliefs that are most important to human life only required a bare-bones, common-sense metaphysical grounding. More advanced and complicated ruminations on the higher structures of reality might be interesting, but we shouldn't invest too much in them, given the limits of our ability to understand such matters – and their irrelevance, much of the time, to the questions that Locke thought really mattered in life: How should I live? What are my duties? Why did God make me? And most importantly, since I'm sinful and God is righteous, "what must I do to be saved?"[101]

This was of much more than merely academic importance. The old epistemology, which had dominated the universities, greatly limited empirical science and other new fields of inquiry. Locke comments in the *Essay Concerning Human Understanding* that he feels very inferior to the great scientific minds of the day, like his friend Isaac Newton or his mentor Robert Boyle. He feels honored, he writes, to be employed as a lowly workman in their service, by "clearing the ground a little, and removing some of the rubbish" that was blocking the roads they needed to travel – rubbish produced equally by medieval monks and Enlightenment rationalists (E Epistle, 10).

But at least as important as that was Locke's reorientation of epistemology toward solving the practical problems of moral and religious life in a society characterized by intense conflict over belief. While other epistemologists tended to ignore the practical realm, Locke was focused on constructing an ethical system for responsible belief regulation.

By emphasizing the imperative of every individual mind to search for truth, he constructed a framework for conceiving of all religious and philosophical systems as things that had to be pursued voluntarily, by those who really wanted to find out whether truth might be found there, in order to be meaningful or beneficial. This, alone, had a transformative impact that it would be difficult to overstate.

Obviously it was not a new idea that people *ought* to pursue these things voluntarily. The advocates of each system had always thought that everyone ought to want to follow it. Nor was it new to say that these things would only provide their greatest and most lasting benefits to those who pursued them voluntarily.

But the idea that religious and philosophical systems had no value at all – that they were, in fact, positively harmful – when imposed on people who weren't persuaded by them had not previously made much progress. In classical Greece and Rome, it had flourished among the philosophers, but had no influence outside that small circle. The philosophers did their "search for truth" thing, and the world more or less ignored them. In later ages, expanding this approach to society at large had been toyed with – we find Augustine remarking that "no one is ... to be compelled to embrace the faith against his will," and other figures after him occasionally making similar gestures.[102] From time to time we find someone making a fully worked-out case for it.[103] However, the idea did not grow and thrive in practice until modernity, and Locke's epistemology of the universal search for truth was one of the major reasons it finally took root.

Closely related to this is Locke's emphasis on the limitations of the human mind, and on maintaining the appropriate "degrees of assent" in our beliefs. The predominant mode of belief and argument before Locke was to focus almost exclusively on the distinction between truth and falsehood. Locke reshaped public discourse on a new set of terms – what is knowable with full certainty, knowable with greater certainty, knowable with less certainty, and not knowable at all.

This did as much as anything to defuse conflict over beliefs, because it provided a responsible and intelligible way for people to treat some of their beliefs as subject to uncertainty without undermining all of their beliefs. To return to the striking example from Locke's hometown in Chapter 1, the question of whether playing sports is permissible on Sunday can be distinguished from the question of whether Christianity is true. Locke's epistemology helped people admit that reasonable Christians can honestly read their Bibles and honestly come to different conclusions about sports on Sunday, because it showed them with greater clarity that they could admit this without implying any uncertainty about the truth of Christianity itself.

ii. FAITH THAT WORKS BY LOVE – LOCKE'S RELIGIOUS LEGACY

But epistemology was not the only argument Locke offered for peaceful coexistence. Locke believed that religious toleration was not only the rational approach, but was commanded in revelation. God had spoken on this point not only through our natural reason, but through his written word.

If toleration had been justified merely on grounds of technical philosophy, it would only have been convincing to those who looked to technical philosophy to guide their lives. As widely read and as dramatically influential as Locke's *Essay* was, it's hard to imagine the *Essay* alone carrying the cause of toleration to triumph. The *Essay* prepares the ground for toleration by reorienting the way people think about their beliefs. However, preparing the ground doesn't get you anything but an empty plot of land; after preparing, you have to build.

Locke's *Letter Concerning Toleration*, making the case for broad-ranging religious toleration on explicitly Christian grounds by drawing on scripture and Christian theology, is one of the most influential and transformative documents in Christian history. Others had made the case for toleration many times before; geopolitical events were creating a more receptive audience for the message, and opening opportunities to put it into practice; and others besides Locke did much work to spread it. But no single document even compares in importance with the *Letter*. Its nearly overnight success – in nations across the face of Europe, and crossing the sectarian lines that usually divided people over religion – galvanized support for toleration into a movement.

The *Letter* provided the turning point. Philosophers, theologians and politicians could no longer simply play around with the idea of toleration, or espouse it in principle only to neglect it in practice. Europe had been through the cycle of religious violence just enough times to push just enough people to be just sick and tired enough of it all to try something radically new.

And Locke did not just change the fortunes of the movement for toleration; he changed the way toleration was understood. For most of human history, most (though not all) supporters of religious toleration conceived of it as merely a prudent policy. Thanks in large part to Locke, that kind of argument for toleration began taking a backseat to a new kind of argument – one that demanded toleration as a basic necessity of justice, decency, and Christian love of neighbor. Before, advocates of toleration had said, in effect, "yes, we have the right to persecute these people for their beliefs, but it's a lot more trouble than it's worth. Everything will be so much easier if we just ignore them." Now, they were saying, "nothing could be more offensive to God or more destructive of the moral laws politics must uphold than persecuting people in the name of faith. Faith works by love."

As a result, this was not simply a turning point on one issue. This was a fundamental change in how we conceive of the relationship between religion and politics. It was not enough simply to refrain from killing, torturing, and imprisoning people for their beliefs. Toleration now implied a whole new understanding of what it meant to be a citizen and a member of society – namely, that membership in society was conditioned on obedience to the basic laws of civilized behavior, not religious beliefs and practices as such.

The turning point on religious toleration was a turning point for the whole world. The "modern" world began with this reconceptualization of religion and politics. It changes the entire landscape – the structure of virtually all political and social institutions.

iii.   MORAL CONSENSUS – LOCKE'S POLITICAL LEGACY

A new political world requires a new political philosophy. To a large extent, that's why the religious fragmentation that occurred after the Reformation led to so much bloodshed; people were still using a political philosophy that assumed a shared faith in society when there was no longer such a shared faith.

Locke was far from the only political philosopher seeking to cope with the breakdown of the old social order after the Reformation. But he was the most successful. He provided a framework for how to justify the political system and legitimize political action without relying on a shared religion, and did so in a way that was persuasive across most sectarian boundaries because it appealed to natural reason.

Traditionally, medieval thinkers had justified an extensive interdependence of church and state by appealing to the factor they shared in common: morality. It was true, they agreed, that the saving of souls and other matters pertaining to eternal life had been entrusted by God wholly to the church, and administration of civil laws to govern matters pertaining to life in this world had been entrusted wholly to the state. But the state requires a moral basis to justify its actions, they argued, and you cannot separate morality from God.

Locke agreed that the state needs a moral basis, and that you cannot separate morality from God. Without a moral basis, politics is reduced to the brutality of mere power. If there is no absolute, objective and verifiable standard of what is morally right in politics, then the political order is nothing but one set of people forcibly imposing its preferences upon another set of people, not for any legitimate reason but simply because they prefer it. And even a few moments' thought will show that the question of what is right and wrong cannot be separated from the question of what kind of universe we live in and what kind of beings we are – which are, ultimately, questions about religion.

But Locke thought the medieval natural law thinkers had not taken seriously enough their idea that all people know the basics of right and wrong because God has made us in such a way that we're bound to discover them. The rules of interpersonal justice – don't kill, don't steal, keep your promises, etc. – are shared among all humanity because they're rooted in human nature.

Locke argued that if this was so, the state doesn't need a basis in any particular religion. It has all the justification it needs in natural reason.

Another thing that made Locke's natural law theory stand out from earlier approaches is the minimalism of its content. Locke didn't attempt to construct an extensive moral code from natural reason, as most previous natural law thinkers had done. He selected the one rule – human life is to be preserved, because it's wrong to treat human beings like property – that he thought was clearly and unmistakably engraved in human nature.

This minimal-content approach allowed Locke to build consensus across the lines of religious belief. Everyone agrees that things like murder and theft should be against the law; Locke provides a cogent explanation as to why. By sticking to the moral principles everyone agrees on, and showing that this area of moral consensus is sufficient to justify the political order, Locke eliminates the need for divisive and ruinous political conflicts over religion.

iv. WHAT CAME NEXT

Since it began, the modern era has seen continual, dramatic, and deep-seated change. All ages do – a man lifted out of the ninth century and put down in the fourteenth century would have been shocked and dumbfounded by much of what he saw. But the changes we've seen in modernity since its arrival have probably surpassed those of any previous era.

While it would be impossible to list even all of the most important of these changes, some of the ones that bear most immediately on Locke's legacy include:

- The rapid development of a more detailed and cogent philosophy of political revolution led to a significant increase in the frequency of revolutions. The period following Locke's ascendance is sometimes referred to as the "age of revolutions." (Some people limit that designation to a period of roughly a century or so; others think the age of revolutions is only just beginning.)
- A key element that emerged in Enlightenment political philosophy was the attempt to systematically analyze the operation of political institutions, to see what kinds of institutions work best. In *The Federalist Papers*, Alexander Hamilton called this "the science of politics."[104] Some important political ideologies arose from the intersection of Locke's philosophy of the moral foundations of politics with constitutional theories produced by this movement.
- The rejection of revealed religion in favor of believing only what natural reason could show us became much more influential, especially in continental Europe. Ironically, although Locke had worked to oppose such rationalism in books like *The Reasonableness of Christianity as Revealed in the Scriptures*, his political philosophy helped remove obstacles to it by removing revealed religion from the shared basis of social and political life.
- Related to the rise of rationalism was the rising influence of theories holding that morality need not be grounded in God or anything else transcendent. In its more militant forms, rationalism held that belief in revealed religion, far from benefiting society by providing a source of commitment to moral goodness, was harmful and dangerous to society.
- Starting with the Romantic movement, sparked by Jean-Jacques Rousseau in the mid-eighteenth century, there has been a continual series of reactions against the removal of ultimate meaning from the political sphere. While medieval theory had always held that the ultimate meaning and purpose of life was not to be found

in politics, the modern approach – typified by Locke – reduced the dignity and importance of politics even further. The Romantics, and a series of movements after them (ranging from Hegelian Idealists to Marxists to fascists and nihilists to Islamists) hold out visions of achieving a redemptive new life-meaning through transformative political action. These movements, while diverse in many other ways, are always religious or quasi-religious in nature, and understand themselves centrally as challenges to Christianity – which, they believe, holds humanity back from the drastic socio-political transformation it needs by teaching it to seek redemption outside of worldly affairs.

- The focus on "ideas" inside the mind in Locke's epistemology heralded a new turn in epistemology, but this approach came to be divorced from Locke's firm and unshakeable confidence that it was rational to assume that ideas arising from sensation are systematically reliable. Much later epistemology would cut off reason entirely from the world outside the mind, either by denying that we could really know anything about what was outside the mind (as in the skepticism of David Hume) or by radically separating things outside the mind from our subjective experiences of them (as in Immanuel Kant). This paved the way for numerous intellectual developments, including the rise of openly solipsistic and anti-rational ideologies.

- Democracy came to be elevated as a fundamental requirement of political legitimacy. In Locke's theory, what matters is not democracy as such but rule by consent rather than force – and people can consent to any form of government. The appropriate form of government depends on the local situation of every society. Locke does assert Parliament's supremacy over the king, but not because it's democratic; he favors Parliament because it's the legislature, and he thinks the legislative power is inherently the supreme seat of any government's authority.

- Alternative political ideologies arose that support the same basic political outcomes as the Lockean approach – religious toleration, rule by consent, etc. – but starting from different philosophical premises. Ever since Edmund Burke's reaction against the French Revolution, political traditionalism has provided an alternative justification (mostly associated with the political right) for basically the same kind of state Locke envisions. And John Stuart Mill's development of a more moderate form of utilitarianism, combined with his conception of politics as fundamentally shaped by the competing imperatives progress and conservation, has provided yet another justification (mostly associated with the political left).

But perhaps the most important change has been the exposure of an inherent problem in Locke's philosophy itself – his blindness to the problem of producing the moral consensus on which his philosophy relies so heavily.

v. THE BREAKDOWN OF MORAL CONSENSUS

Throughout his writings, Locke takes it for granted that society will not have difficulty producing broad agreement, across all belief groups, for the fundamental moral laws that govern society. Given the general principles on which his theory is based, this may seem like a natural assumption for him to make. The whole idea of natural law is that this basic moral knowledge is available to everyone, and appeals to it will find support across all groups.

But politics requires the development of moral laws beyond mere bare-bones abstractions like "don't kill" and "don't steal." We need specifics. We need definitions and clarifications. We need applications and case law. Locke himself says that one of the defects of the state of nature would be the absence of "an established, settled, known law, received and allowed by common consent to be the standard of right and wrong, and the measure to decide all controversies between them" (T II.124, 178). In context, he seems to be talking not about the natural law (knowledge of which is not lacking in the state of nature) but a written legal code to provide us with a shared set of specific parameters for how to apply the natural law to particular cases.

The problem is, people don't naturally agree on these specifics as much as they naturally agree on the basics in the abstract. Locke treats this exclusively as a problem of selfish bias – people disagree about specific applications of the natural law because everyone wants it applied in the way that is advantageous to him or her. That's why establishing a government solves the problem for Locke. But people disagree about these applications even apart from selfish bias. The natural level of consensus on moral matters decreases the further you go down the continuum from abstract generalities to hard specifics.

Examples of this problem from contemporary politics occur almost immediately if we think about the two rules just mentioned – not killing and not stealing. What counts as killing? Is abortion killing? In all cases or only in some? And as to stealing, where do we draw the line between unseemly greed and outright theft when it comes to some of the shady things that were done in the buildup to the 2008 financial crisis? What kinds of economic behaviors should be punishable? And how much government involvement in the economy is permissible? The U.S. government engineered a special bankruptcy process for General Motors in 2009 that excluded many of the company's debt-holders from receiving bankruptcy proceeds to which they had been legally entitled. Was that theft?

To some extent this disagreement is fueled by the influence of ideologies in direct contradiction to Locke's. Part of what makes people disagree about what counts as theft is that people disagree over what counts as property, or to what extent property rights are a creation of government rather than a natural phenomenon. To this extent, the problem is not an incoherence in Locke but simply a conflict between Lockean and non-Lockean views of politics.

But this doesn't get Locke all the way off the hook. For one thing, not all these disagreements are of the nature. Some of them directly implicate the kind of metaphysics Locke says should be politically irrelevant. Abortion is again the obvious example. What is a human being? Any distinct organism of the species *Homo sapiens*? Or only those that meet certain criteria? These are exactly the kind of questions Locke warns us in the *Essay* not to spend too much of our time worrying about. In the *Essay* he repeatedly uses this very issue – trying to define what is or is not a human being – as an example illustrating the pointless speculations of the scholastics (see E III.6.22, 450; III.10.22, 503; IV.4.12, 447; IV.4.14–16, 569–573; and IV.7.16–17, 606–607). But we have discovered that we cannot have a politics that doesn't ask these questions. Love it or hate it, metaphysics matters.

And even where these problems do arise from ideologies in direct contradiction to Locke's, that phenomenon is one Locke ought to have foreseen and had an answer for. No political philosopher has any right to expect that the whole world will fall down and adopt his philosophy. And of all political philosophers, Locke stresses more than anyone the persistent intractability of disagreements about belief. He of all people should have foreseen that moral consensus would not maintain itself.

vi. THE TWENTY-FIRST CENTURY – EITHER NEO-LOCKEAN OR PRE-LOCKEAN

No doubt every age has its share of divisive controversies. Yet in our time we seem to be undergoing a much more fundamental breakdown of consensus about the political rules of right and wrong than most ages, or even any age, have seen in the past. We seem to be disagreeing not just about particular issues, but about fundamental models of legitimacy. The United States, for example – to paint with a broad brush for a moment – seems to be divided roughly in half between those of a broadly Lockean bent and those who think about politics roughly the way Mill did. How long can such a divided house stand?

Perhaps this is only a trick of perspective. Perhaps – if only we could see with their eyes – the disagreements about permitting sports on Sunday in seventeenth-century England felt to them to be as much a fundamental division between worldviews as divisions over abortion or government ownership of major corporations feel that way to us. Certainly they spoke and acted as though they thought sports on Sunday was an issue of extremely grave importance. Yet it's hard to believe, surveying the depth and breadth of our divisions, that we aren't witnessing something much more fundamental.

What makes our divisions so much deeper – or, at least, seem that way – is that we lack even a shared conceptual framework to define the debate. We don't even have the same ideas about what it is that we're disagreeing about. In seventeenth-century England, proponents and opponents of permitting sports on Sunday at least had a framework of shared moral commitments within which that debate took place.

In the absence of a shared religion, our moral disagreements go "all the way down" – perhaps not always in actuality, but at least in potential. In our culture wars, people often express frustration at the feeling that we're shouting at each other but not successfully communicating. If so, that's because communication requires a shared set of concepts about which and through which we communicate. We have to agree to a certain extent even before we can succeed in disagreeing. Without that, we can only make noise – or apply brute force.

And yet it seems unlikely that anything new will come to replace the broadly Lockean lines of our civilization. We still face the same old dilemma Locke did. On the one hand, going back to politics based on an enforced community religion would be wrong, for all the same reasons Locke originally gave us. On the other, any politics not based on some kind of shared concept of right and wrong would be based on nothing at all but the brutalistic assertion of power for its own sake. To thread this needle, we need to maintain moral consensus without religious consensus. Locke may not have equipped us to do that, but it's hard to see any alternative to making the attempt.

In short, if we don't find some kind of neo-Lockeanism – starting from something like Locke but adding some account of how to build moral consensus in the absence of religious consensus – we are likely to end up not with something newer than Locke but with something older. We may fall back into the confessional-state model; we might continue to tolerate dissent, but one religious (or quasi-religious) viewpoint would be officially endorsed, and policy would be made on that basis. Or we may fall back into mere cynical *realpolitik*; the state may simply give up trying to justify itself morally. Plenty of societies in human history have embraced both models, and indeed both are easily visible in the world around us today. There's no reason to think either of them couldn't make a comeback in the western, or even the English-speaking, world.

If we are especially ill-favored, we may get both at once. The rudimentary beginnings of such an outcome are already clearly visible on both sides of the divide. In both "conservative" and "progressive" circles, some people demand policy that imposes their views on others, and when challenged, appeal not to the rightness of the policy but to the majority support it allegedly enjoys. As one such figure succinctly puts it: "Someone's values are going to prevail. Why not ours? Whose country is it, anyway?"[105] This is an amoral assertion of mere power, made in the service of a superficially moral vision.

But better things may also be hoped for. When confronted with either explicit political confessionalism or explicit political cynicism, large majorities still draw back – usually in horror. By and large, we may not yet have figured out how to cope with our disagreements effectively, but we do know we don't want to stamp them out by force. That spirit is Locke's greatest legacy, and as long as it endures, we will owe him thanks for it.

NOTES

1   Bodleian Library manuscripts, Locke c. 28 f.2a; quoted in Maurice Cranston, *John Locke: A Biography*, New York: Oxford University Press, 1957.

2   Scholars take a variety of views on what are the most fundamental defining characteristics of "modernity." Some point to the reorganization of social conditions caused by advances of technology. However, dramatic technological advances – accompanied by equally dramatic reorganizations of society – occurred during many ancient periods (think of what the aqueduct and road improvements did for Rome) and, even more, throughout the Middle Ages. I believe the emphasis on technology as the defining characteristic of modernity largely stems from widespread ignorance (even among scholars) of the extent and impact of technological change during premodern periods, combined with the strong impression made on the mind by the extraordinary acceleration of technological change during the last few decades. Most other views about modernity center on a change in the role of religion. Two general schools of thought seem to dominate, one holding that the influence of religion declined (the "secularization thesis") and the other holding that the role of religion in society changed dramatically without declining. Locke is central to the story in either version.

3   Some of the more important works contributing to this argument are C.B. Macpherson, *The Political Theory of Possessive Individualism*, London: Oxford University Press, 1962; John Dunn, *The Political Thought of John Locke*, Cambridge: Cambridge University Press, 1969; James Tully, *An Approach to Political Philosophy: Locke in Contexts*, Cambridge: Cambridge University Press, 1984; Richard Ashcraft, *Revolutionary Politics and Locke's Two Treatises of Government*, Princeton: Princeton University Press, 1986; Ruth Grant, *John Locke's Liberalism*, Chicago: University of Chicago Press, 1987; John Marshall, *John Locke: Resistance, Religion and Responsibility*, Cambridge: Cambridge University Press, 1994; Nicholas Wolterstorff, *John Locke and the Ethics of Belief*, Cambridge: Cambridge University Press, 1996; Francis Oakley, "Locke, Natural Law, and God – Again," *History of*

Political Thought 18 (1997): 624–651; Nicholas Jolley, *Locke: His Philosophical Thought*, London: Oxford University Press, 1999; Jeremy Waldron, *God, Locke, and Equality*, Cambridge: Cambridge University Press, 2002. Closely related to this topic is the ongoing debate over Leo Strauss's approach to Locke; for extensive discussion and citations on that debate see Greg Forster, *John Locke's Politics of Moral Consensus*, Cambridge: Cambridge University Press, 2005.

4   Wolterstorff, *Ethics of Belief*, p. xii.

5   Augustine, *Against the Book of Petilian the Donatist*, 2.84.

6   Augustine, *City of God*, 19.12.

7   Three excellent sources on medieval theology are Ewart Lewis, ed., *Medieval Political Ideas*, New York: Knopf, 1954, 2 volumes; Paul Sigmund, ed., *St. Thomas Aquinas on Politics and Ethics*, New York: Norton, 1988; and Oliver O'Donovan and Joan Lockwood O'Donovan, eds., *From Irenaeus to Grotius: A Sourcebook in Christian Political Thought*, Grand Rapids: Eerdmans, 1999.

8   As we will see in Chapter 3, the specific arguments over toleration for Catholics in 1689 England were actually much more complicated than this, because certain specific historical events had led most English Protestants to think that following Catholicism in England was not only religious heresy but also a form of civil treason. However, the précis given here is an accurate outline of the Lockean philosophy of religious toleration in its general form, and it is worth remembering that Locke himself intended this philosophy for audiences in all of Europe, not just for England. The *Letter Concerning Toleration* is written not in English, but in Latin. Locke did not even produce an English version of the *Letter* – the English edition in consistent use from 1689 to the present day comes from an English publisher who took Locke's original Latin and translated it.

9   Two of the more important examples of such direct side-taking are his frontal assault on "innate principles" and other Cartesian epistemology in the *Essay Concerning Human Understanding* and his thinly veiled swipes at the Roman Catholic Church in the *Letter Concerning Toleration*. Notice, though, that he only brings up these quarrels where they are necessary to the argument; his hostility toward Rome is kept out of the *Essay*, his critique of Descartes is kept out of the *Letter*, and both are kept out of the *Two Treatises of Government*. This is more significant than it may at first seem – for example, one of the major causes of the success of the *Two Treatises* is probably its construction of a natural law argument that was equally appealing to those who did and did not believe that the natural law is an innate idea. See Forster, *Moral Consensus*, pp. 30–32 and 220–225.

10 For more information on Christian political thought and controversies before the Reformation, see Ewart Lewis, ed., *Medieval Political Ideas*, New York: Knopf, 1954, 2 volumes; and Oliver O'Donovan and Joan Lockwood O'Donovan, eds., *From Irenaeus to Grotius: A Sourcebook in Christian Political Thought*, Grand Rapids: Eerdmans, 1999.

NOTES

11 Martin Luther, *On Secular Authority*, part II.
12 For a comprehensive overview of the Reformation see Diarmid McCulloch, *The Reformation*, New York: Penguin Books, 2005.
13 For more on this topic see Greg Forster, *The Contested Public Square*, Downer's Grove, IL: InterVarsity Press, 2008, pp. 107–141.
14 Hans Aarsleff, "Locke's Influence," in *The Cambridge Companion to Locke*, ed. Vere Chappell, Cambridge: Cambridge University Press, 1994, p. 254.
15 Maurice Cranston, *John Locke: A Biography*, New York: Oxford University Press, 1957, pp. 11–12. This chapter draws extensively from Cranton's account, which remains the standard biography of Locke.
16 See John Marshall, *John Locke: Resistance, Religion and Responsibility*, New York: Cambridge University Press, 1994, p. xix.
17 See Cranston, *John Locke*, p. 74.
18 See Cranston, *John Locke*, p. 74.
19 See J.R. Milton, "Locke's Life and Times," in *Cambridge Companion*, p. 6.
20 Quoted in Cranston, *John Locke*, p. 82.
21 Quoted in Cranston, *John Locke*, p. 82.
22 See Cranston, *John Locke*, pp. 47–56 and 84–87. Locke and his paramour(s) signed their love-notes with pseudonyms, and Locke received such letters in Cleves signed with several different pseudonyms, which may mean he had multiple correspondents – but there is also some reason to believe the letters may have come from the same woman using different pseudonyms. One of these letters takes the form of a satirical newsletter. It notes that the Dutch are sending all their English prisoners of war back home, since they consume food but do no work, and expresses a wish that the Germans in Cleves might observe the same principle regarding English diplomats. It also notes complaints coming from the English government that its diplomats abroad don't send home enough reports because they spend too much time writing letters to their mistresses. Recalling all the diplomats home, the newsletter notes, would be an effective way to end this flagrant abuse of the English taxpayer.
23 See Cranston, *John Locke*, pp. 75–76 and 100–103.
24 Cranston (*John Locke*, p. 111) asserts that Locke had already become a full supporter of toleration even before meeting Ashley, but doesn't say on what evidence this assertion is based. In any event, Cranston stresses that Ashley's influence was the pivotal factor in transforming Locke into an active champion of toleration by moving it from a sideline to a centerpiece of Locke's intellectual interests, and helping him develop a more clear and systematic understanding of the subject.
25 See Richard Ashcraft, *Revolutionary Politics and Locke's Two Treatises of Government*, Princeton: Princeton University Press, 1986, pp. 17–20 and 115–116.
26 See Marshall, *Resistance, Religion and Responsibility*, p. 357.
27 See Cranston, *John Locke*, p. 15.
28 See Cranston, *John Locke*, p. 185.

29 John Marshall, "John Locke on Property and God: A Historical Perspective," delivered to the Annual Meeting of the American Political Science Association, 2008.

30 See "Chronology of His Times," in *Two Treatises of Government*, ed. Mark Goldie, London: Everyman, 1993, p. xi.

31 David Wootton, "Introduction," in *Political Writings of John Locke*, New York: Penguin Books, pp. 49–89. Perhaps the most persuasive part of Wootton's case is the fact that one section of the *First Treatise* appears (from the markings used by printers to keep track of page groupings) to have been a late insertion. This section just happens to be the only portion of the *First Treatise* that reflects Tyrrell in much the same way the *Second Treatise* does. Also of evidentiary value are letters from Tyrrell to Locke in which Tyrrell seems to suggest that Locke should have acknowledged a debt to his ideas.

32 See especially John Dunn, *The Political Thought of John Locke*, New York: Cambridge University Press, 1969.

33 See Francis Oakley, "Locke, Natural Law and God – Again," *History of Political Thought* 18 (1997): 624–651; and James Tully, *A Discourse on Property*, Cambridge: Cambridge University Press, 1980.

34 Tyrrell thinks that contracts entered into under duress are morally obligatory (and hence conquerors can obtain political sovereignty over the people they conquer) and that when people join a society they submit their property rights entirely to the control of society (and hence there are no hard and fast limits on the extent to which it can be regulated or taxed). Locke forcefully rebuts both of these more conservative premises in the *Second Treatise* (see T II.175–196, 205–215; and II.140,187 and II.142, 188).

35 Dating the composition of the *Two Treatises* has been the subject of some controversy, but a consensus has emerged that it was probably substantially composed during the Exclusion Crisis, before Locke left England. See Richard Ashcraft, "Simple Objections and Complex Reality: Theorizing Political Radicalism in Seventeenth-Century England," *Political Studies* 40 (1992): 99–115; and Wootton, "Introduction."

36 See Cranston, *John Locke*, pp. 215–219, 236–238. Their relationship, which had always been a lively intellectual friendship, survived the end of its romantic aspect; after his return from exile, Locke quickly discovered that his ill health prevented him from living in London, and Cudworth – now Lady Masham – invited him to rent rooms in her family's country estate. This he did, and lived there from 1690 through his death in 1704. They two remained very close; Lady Masham's husband was not the sort of man who could satisfy her restless intellectual curiosity (see p. 344). When Locke died, Lady Masham was reading him psalms.

37 Some consider his silence on these crucial questions as evidence that he held unorthodox views on them, but this is unwarranted. He may have been undecided. Given his emphasis on the human mind's limited

ability to understand higher metaphysical phenomena, it would not be at all surprising if he thought these questions were above human capacity to grasp; some comments in his book *The Reasonableness of Christianity* suggest this. It is even possible he were decided for the orthodox position, but remained silent for other reasons (such as to avoid the possibility of being prosecuted for defending orthodox positions in a way the religious authorities didn't approve of). For an extended discussion of this question see Greg Forster, *John Locke's Politics of Moral Consensus*, Cambridge: Cambridge University Press, 2005, pp. 150–159.

38 Cranston, *John Locke*, p. 305.
39 See Peter Nidditch, "Introduction," in *An Essay Concerning Human Understanding*, Oxford: Clarendon Press, 1975, p. xvi.
40 For a full discussion of the historical context of the *Reasonableness* and Locke's purposes in writing it, see Forster, *Moral Consensus*, pp. 130–135.
41 See Richard Ashcraft, *Revolutionary Politics and Locke's Two Treatises of Government*, Princeton: Princeton University Press, 1986, pp. 109–110; and Nicholas Wolterstorff, "Locke's Philosophy of Religion," in *The Cambridge Companion to Locke*, ed. Vere Chappell, Cambridge: Cambridge University Press, 1994, p. 174.
42 See Ashcraft, *Revolutionary Politics*, pp. 105–106.
43 See J.R. Milton, "Locke's Life and Times," in *Cambridge Companion*, p. 6.
44 See Milton, "Locke's Life," pp. 10–11.
45 Nicholas Wolterstorff, *John Locke and the Ethics of Belief*, Cambridge: Cambridge University Press, 1996.
46 On Locke and the controversies in his time over natural science, see especially Nicholas Jolley, *Locke: His Philosophical Thought*, New York: Oxford University Press, 1999.
47 For example, when Augustine takes up the subject of politics in Book XIX of *The City of God*, he begins by saying that he will proceed "not merely by appealing to divine authority, but also by employing such powers of reason as we can apply for the benefit of unbelievers" (Augustine, *The City of God*, New York: Penguin Books, 1984, p. 843).
48 For example, this definition of "faith" is defended in C.S. Lewis's *Mere Christianity* (in *The Complete C.S. Lewis Signature Classics*, San Francisco: Harper, 2002, pp. 77–79), which is widely regarded as a good introductory summary of what Christianity has historically taught.
49 Wolterstorff, *Ethics of Belief*, p. xii.
50 See Greg Forster and Kim Ian Parker, "'Men Being Partial to Themselves': Human Selfishness in Locke's *Two Treatises*," *Politics and Religion* (2008): 169–199.
51 See Jolley, *Philosophical Thought*, p. 37.
52 See Vere Chappell, "Introduction," in *Cambridge Companion*, p. 28.
53 See John Yolton, *John Locke and the Way of Ideas*, London: Oxford University Press, 1956, pp. 86–98; and Chappell, "Introduction," p. 26.

54 See Jolley, *Philosophical Thought*, pp. 80–99.
55 This chapter was one of the last additions to the *Essay*, first appearing in the fourth edition. This is a reflection of its systematic importance; in it, Locke concisely summarizes how the lengthy account of ideas in Book II connects to the processes of belief formation considered in Book IV – fundamentally, we form beliefs by associating ideas.
56 For more on Locke's role in the extremely controversial debates in Locke's time between the medieval essentialism of the university faculties and the "corpuscularian hypothesis" of the Enlightenment scientists of the Royal Society, see Edwin McCann, "Locke's Philosophy of Body," in *Cambridge Companion*, pp. 56–88; and Jolley, *Philosophical Thought*, pp. 55–79.
57 See Francis Oakley, "Locke, Natural Law and God – Again," *History of Political Thought* 18 (1997): 624–51, pp. 628 and 636.
58 See for example Wolterstorff, *Ethics of Belief*.
59 Steven Forde, "Natural Law, Theology and Morality in Locke," *American Journal of Political Science* 45 (2001): 396–409, p. 403; see also pp. 402 and 408.
60 Augustine, *The City of God*, New York: Penguin Books, 1984, p. 843.
61 For an overview of Locke's theology and the scholarly debates surrounding it, see Greg Forster, *John Locke's Politics of Moral Consensus*, Cambridge: Cambridge University Press, 2005, pp. 128–166.
62 There is one school of thought that takes Locke's professions of religious belief to be dishonest, but this is extremely difficult to square with the evidence; for a discussion of this debate see Forster, *Moral Consensus*.
63 Both schools can create paradoxes if they take their ideas too far. The intellectualists must be careful not to make goodness something that God merely perceives, implying that "the good" exists prior to God, and God is subordinate to it; the voluntarists must be careful not to make goodness merely whatever God commands, implying that there is no "goodness" within God himself. Historically, orthodox Christian theologians have agreed that "the good" is a characteristic of God, neither merely perceived by him nor merely commanded by him. Yet the difference between the two schools remains, and remains important.
64 For further discussion on Locke's voluntarism and its significance, see Nicholas Wolterstorff, *John Locke and the Ethics of Belief*, Cambridge: Cambridge University Press, 1996, p. 138; Francis Oakley, "Locke, Natural Law, and God – Again," *History of Political Thought* 18 (1997): 624–651; and Forster, *Moral Consensus*, pp. 103–105 and 177–182.
65 John Locke, *A Discourse of Miracles*, in *The Reasonableness of Christianity, with A Discourse of Miracles and part of A Third Letter on Toleration*, ed. I.T. Ramsey, Stanford: Stanford University Press, 1958, p. 80.
66 The process of examining the evidence for miracles gives rise to some special epistemological concerns, which Locke addressed in his posthumously published short treatise *A Discourse on Miracles* (cited above). Locke's general approach to the epistemology of miracles mirrors that

of many other Christian philosophers; see for example C.S. Lewis, *Miracles: A Preliminary Study*, London: G. Bles, 1947.
67 See Nicholas Wolterstorff, *John Locke and the Ethics of Belief*, Cambridge: Cambridge University Press, 1996, pp. 132–133.
68 See Forster, *Moral Consensus*, pp. 135–140.
69 See Forster, *Moral Consensus*, pp. 159–165.
70 See Forster, *Moral Consensus*, pp. 148–160.
71 In commenting on the case of a Muslim who owes his political allegiance to a hostile foreign power, Locke makes it clear that he thinks the same principle excludes toleration for Roman Catholics in England, given that the papacy had told English Catholics in the previous century that they didn't need to obey the English government (see Chapter 1). Elsewhere in the *Letter*, however, in a comment directed at the revocation of toleration for Protestants in France, he remarks that Roman Catholic and Calvinist worship should be equally permitted (see L 76, 55). This may suggest that Locke (unlike most Whigs) sees nothing inherently threatening to freedom in Roman Catholicism; he just thinks Catholicism is a threat to freedom in England because of the papacy's attempt to dethrone Protestant English monarchs.
72 For an overview of the history of natural law from its roots in Greco-Roman thought to the twentieth century, see Greg Forster, *The Contested Public Square*, Downer's Grove, IL: InterVarsity Press, 2008.
73 See Aristotle, *Nichomachean Ethics*, trans. David Ross, J.L. Ackrill and J.O. Urmson, New York: Oxford University Press, 1992, pp. 4–24 (Book I, Sections 4–12).
74 See John Marshall, *John Locke: Resistance, Religion and Responsibility*, Cambridge: Cambridge University Press, 1994, pp. 299–326.
75 See Forster, *Contested Public Square*, pp. 87–90.
76 W.M. Spellman, *John Locke and the Problem of Depravity*, Oxford: Clarendon Press, 1988, pp. 119–120.
77 See Aristotle, *Ethics*, pp. 14 and 19–22 (Book I, Sections 7 and 10).
78 See Greg Forster, *John Locke's Politics of Moral Consensus*, Cambridge: Cambridge University Press, 2005, p. 199.
79 On Locke's account of pleasure and pain see Forster, *Moral Consensus*, pp. 195–198.
80 On Locke and slavery, both as a concept and as a practice, see James Farr, " 'So Vile and Miserable an Estate': The Problem of Slavery in Locke's Political Thought," *Political Theory* 14 (1986): 263–289.
81 See Ewart Lewis, ed., *Medieval Political Ideas*, New York: Knopf, 1954, 2 volumes; and Oliver O'Donovan and Joan Lockwood O'Donovan, eds., *From Irenaeus to Grotius: A Sourcebook in Christian Political Thought*, Grand Rapids: Eerdmans, 1999.
82 See Charles Tarlton, "A Rope of Sand: Interpreting Locke's *First Treatise of Government*," in *John Locke: Critical Assessments*, ed. Richard Ashcraft, New York: Routledge, 1991.

83 On the exegetical argument of the *First Treatise* see Greg Forster, *John Locke's Politics of Moral Consensus*, Cambridge: Cambridge University Press, 2005, pp. 145–148 and 230–239.

84 On Locke's approach to interpretation in the *Essay* and the *First Treatise* see Forster, *Moral Consensus*, pp. 142–148.

85 See Greg Forster, *The Contested Public Square*, Downer's Grove, IL: InterVarsity Press, 2008, p. 184.

86 Locke does believe that if you go back far enough in human history, you will find all people living in a state of nature (see T II.100–101, 165–166). But that is not the main point of his argument.

87 John Dunn sums up the contrast succinctly: "Hobbes's problem is the construction of political society from an ethical vacuum. Locke never faced this problem in the *Two Treatises* because his central premise is precisely the absence of any such vacuum" (John Dunn, *The Political Thought of John Locke*, Cambridge: Cambridge University Press, 1969, p. 79). See also Forster, *Moral Consensus*, pp. 240–242.

88 See Greg Forster and Kim Ian Parker, "'Men Being Partial to Themselves': Human Selfishness in Locke's *Two Treatises*," *Politics and Religion* 1 (2008): 169–199.

89 Locke also briefly mentions a third reason the state of nature is not as advantageous as civil society – in civil society it is possible to pool everyone's strength, so that the enforcement of the natural law carries sufficient strength to overwhelm even the strongest offender – and thus to more effectively deter other offenders as well (see T II.126, 179).

90 Aristotle, *Politics*, trans. T.A. Sinclair and Trevor Saunders, New York: Penguin, 1992, p. 59 (Book I, Section 2).

91 On this argument see Forster, *Moral Consensus*, pp. 248–250.

92 See Charles Tarlton, "A Rope of Sand: Interpreting Locke's *First Treatise of Government*," in *John Locke: Critical Assessments*, ed. Richard Ashcraft, New York: Routledge, 1991.

93 See Richard Ashcraft, *Revolutionary Politics and Locke's Two Treatises of Government*, Princeton: Princeton University Press, 1986, pp. 550–551 and 591.

94 See Aristotle, *Politics*, trans. T.A. Sinclair and Trevor Saunders, New York: Penguin, 1992, p. 264 (Book V, Section 10).

95 Cicero, *On the Republic*, London: Edmund Spettigue, 1841, p. 273.

96 For example, Thomas Aquinas and William of Ockham, the founders of the two great rival schools of thought that dominated the Middle Ages, were agreed on government by consent and the right to rebellion against tyrants. Aquinas writes that a tyrant may be overthrown if he "has violently seized power against the will of his subjects, or has forced them to consent" (Thomas Aquinas, *Commentary on the Sentences of Peter Lombard*; quoted in *St. Thomas Aquinas on Politics and Ethics*, trans. Paul Sigmund, New York: W.W. Norton, 1987, pp. 65–66, n. 8). Ockham writes that "no one should be set over a body of mortals without their choice and consent" (William of Ockham,

Dialogue on the Power of the Emperor and the Pope, in *Medieval Political Ideas,* ed. Ewart Lewis, New York: Knopf, 1954, pp. 79–85).

97 On Locke and slavery, both as a concept and as a practice, see James Farr, " 'So Vile and Miserable an Estate': The Problem of Slavery in Locke's Political Thought," *Political Theory* 14 (1986): 263–289.

98 This is a question on which I have changed my opinion. In my last book, observing the extensive similarities between Locke's ideas and those of the American founding, I was too quick to claim that this proved a direct line of influence (see Greg Forster, *The Contested Public Square,* Downer's Grove, IL: InterVarsity Press, 2008, pp. 195–197). The question will not really be settled until some enterprising historian does an extensive study of it. Unfortunately, the professional divisions between the study of intellectual history and the study of political philosophy have left us with virtually no one qualified to undertake the study – the people who study the intellectual history of the American revolution are almost completely ignorant of the actual content of Locke's philosophy, and vice versa.

99 See Edward Richardson, *Standards and Colors of the American Revolution,* University of Pennsylvania Press, 1982.

100 Hans Aarsleff, "Locke's Influence," in *The Cambridge Companion to Locke,* ed. Vere Chappell, Cambridge: Cambridge University Press, 1994, p. 252.

101 See Acts 16:24–31.

102 Augustine, *Against the Book of Petilian the Donatist,* 2.84.

103 For example, Marsilius of Padua's *Defensor Pacis* or Martin Luther's *On Secular Authority* – although Luther didn't practice what he preached on this point.

104 Alexander Hamilton, James Madison and John Jay, *The Federalist Papers,* New York: Penguin, 1961, p. 72 (Federalist #9).

105 Patrick Buchanan, *Right from the Beginning,* Washington, DC: Regnery, 1990, p. 342.

INDEX

INDEX

Roman Catholicism 5–6, 13, 15, 16–17, 20, 23–24, 28–29, 32, 34, 42, 46, 61, 68, 86, 117–118, 123, 148, 153

Romanticism 141–142

Rome 13, 15, 95, 97, 116, 120, 137, 147

Rousseau, Jean-Jacques 141

Rutherford, Samuel 131

Scholasticism 21, 38, 48, 57–58, 144

Science (see Empirical science)

Scripture (see Bible, the)

Shaftesbury, Earl of (see Cooper, Anthony Ashley)

Sigmund, Paul 148

Socinianism 64, 65

Solon 76

Somerset 19

Spellman, W.M. 153

Spinoza, Baruch 2

Strauss, Leo 148

Tarlton, Charles 153, 154

Theology (see also Bible, the) 2, 35, 39, 61, 63–87, 111, 135, 137–139

  Christology 33, 150–151

  Church, the 5, 9, 13–15, 89

  and innate principles 51, 54–55

  Intellectualism and voluntarism 74–77, 152

  Miracles 78–80, 152–153

  Proofs of God's existence and qualities 73–74

  Soteriology 33, 85–86, 150–151

  and toleration 80–86, 137–139

Tories 30

Tradition 9, 42–43, 45, 47, 49, 68, 71, 80, 88, 94–96, 120, 135, 142–143

Tully, James 147

Two Treatises of Government 31, 34, 35, 78, 91, 93–134, 148, 150, 154

Tyrell, James 31–32, 150

United States 35, 131–133, 144, 145, 155

Utilitarianism 142–143

Vienna 86

Waldron, Jeremy 148

Washington, George 133

Whigs, 30–35, 100, 115

William the Conqueror 109

William of Orange 34–35

Wolterstorff, Nicholas 147, 148, 151, 152, 153

Wootton, David 150

Wrighton 18–19

Yolton, John 151

York, Duke of (see James II)

Zeno 77